'KEEPERS! 19

FULL-BACKS! 20

CENTRE-BACKS! 24

MIDFIELDERS! 26

WINGERS! 30

STRIKERS! 32

THE WORLD'S GREATEST TEAM!

EURO 2008! 38

HOT GOSSIP! 50

PREM SUPER LEAGUE! 58

MEGA RIVALS! 66

TOP TIPS! 70

ACE POSTERS!

VAN NISTELROOY	17
GERRARD	23
TOTTI	29
CRESPO	35
DROGBA	37
RONALDO	45
HENRY	49
FABREGAS	57
KAKA	65
MORIENTES	73
JUNINHO	89
NAKAMURA	93

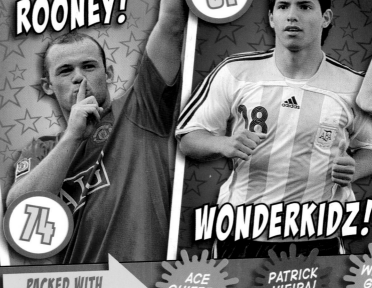

ROONEY! 74

WONDERKIDZ! 81

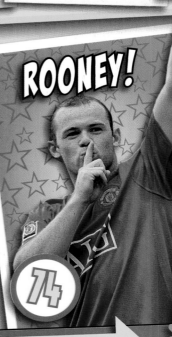
PLANET FOOTY! 12

PACKED WITH FOOTY ACTION!

ACE QUIZZES! 36

PATRICK VIEIRA! 46

WICKED GAME! 90

MATCHMAN CARTOON! 95

PLANET FOOTY!

10 THINGS WE LOVE ABOUT...
LIONEL MES

I'M NOT FOR SALE!

FCB

YOU THE MAN!

1 HE'S BRAVE!

He was only 13 years old when he left his home in Argentina to move to Barcelona! That takes guts!

2 HE'S WELL LOYAL!

Leo could have played for Spain because he's lived there so long – but he turned them down to play for Argentina!

3 HE'S ULTRA POPULAR!

AND I'M STILL TINY!

After scoring a hat-trick against Real Madrid, Messi's big hero Raul came up and congratulated him!

6 HE'S WORTH MILLIONS!

It's written into his contract that any club wanting to buy him will have to offer at least £102 million!

4 HE'S HAD IT TOUGH!

Messi was so small as a boy that he needed special treatment to help him grow! His medicine cost £500 a month!

5 HE'S A BARÇA LEGEND!

He's already won the Champions League, two La Liga titles and two Spanish Super Cups with Barcelona!

FOOTY FACT!

Fulham manager Lawrie Sanchez is the biggest boss in the Prem! He's a huge 6ft 4in tall!

Don't mess!

JT THE SAILOR!

Chelsea captain John Terry spent his honeymoon on Roman Abramovich's £63 million super yacht!

Cheers, Roman!

SÍ!

Barcelona and Argentina trickster Lionel Messi is one of MATCH's fave stars! Check out why he rocks, dudes!

oliver kahn's magic mirror!

Mirror, mirror, on the wall, who's the prettiest of them all?

Er... not you Oliver, you ugly momma!

8 HE CAN PLAY ANYWHERE!

Messi normally plays out wide on the left or right wing — but his favourite position is as the main striker!

7 HE'S A WANTED MAN!

Inter Milan are desperate to buy Messi — and gossips reckon they'll fork out a world record fee to get him!

I'M BETTER!

THE CROUCHYSAURUS!

Hatched: 26 years ago

Natural habitat: Liverpool

Height: Mega tall

Eats: Pasta

Likes: Doing robot dancing

9 HE'S THE NEW MARADONA!

Messi plays just like Argentina legend Diego Maradona when he's flying past defenders with the ball at his feet!

10 HE'S ARGENTINA'S MAIN MAN!

Messi is one of the first names on the team-sheet — even with stars like Tevez and Riquelme in the squad!

FERGIE'S FUNNY FACE!

IT LOOKS LIKE FERGIE'S READY TO BARF! IS IT BECAUSE...
A. HE'S JUST BREATHED IN A STINKY MEGA FART?
B. HE ATE A SPROUT?
C. HE SCOFFED DOWN A WHOLE SELECTION BOX IN 37 SECONDS?

THEO'S SECRET!

Theo Walcott plays football in the garden against his pet dogs!

"I'VE GOT A MASSIVE ALSATIAN AND A LABRADOR! THEY'RE BOTH BRILLIANT - AND VERY TOUGH!"

weird world!
Argentinian side Boca Juniors' stadium is called 'La Bombonera' - which means 'Chocolate Box'!

A ...is for AILTON!
Probably the fattest footballer on the planet! But he's actually quite good and scores loads for German side Duisberg!

B ...is for BREAD & BUTTER!
League football is described as this! It's because it's less glamorous than fancy cup competitions or European matches!

C ...is for CUP!
What teams win - but also what angry managers throw around the dressing room when their team are losing at half-time!

D ...is for DIVE!
MATCH hates players who pretend they've been fouled to win a free-kick or penalty!

I ...is for iPod!
Players travelling on the coach to away games love listening to their MP3 players!

J ...is for JET-HEELED!
Well rapid wingers like Chelsea's Shaun Wright-Phillips and Aaron Lennon of Spurs are often called 'jet-heeled'!

K ...is for KOALA!
MATCH reckons all Australian footballers should have a pet Koala bear! They rock!

THE A-Z OF

O ...is for OLD MAN!
Footy fans love taunting experienced opposition players by singing 'Old man, old man! Old man, old man!'

Q ...is for QUEUEING!
When a defending team is outnumbered by attackers, the strikers are said to be 'queueing up' to score!

S ...is for SLEEP!
Chelsea ace Michael Essien reckons he's got so much energy because he sleeps for 14 hours a day!

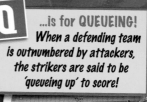

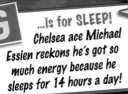

P ...is for PLUM!
When a little team draws a Prem team in a cup competition, commentators will say it's a 'plum draw' - meaning good!

R ...is for ROUTE ONE!
Teams that love playing the long ball up to a big striker play 'route one' football!

T ...is for TWO FEET!
Most people have two feet - but in football terms it means you're good with your left AND your right!

DID YOU KNOW? CHELSEA RIGHT-BACK JULIANO BELLETTI'S MOBILE RINGTONE IS THE SOUND OF HIS SON CRYING!

BIG FAMILY!

Newcastle captain Geremi has 17 brothers and sisters – and his dad had five wives!

E **...is for ERUPT!**
This is what a stadium full of fans does after an important goal has been scored!

F **...is for FLAG HAPPY!**
This refers to a rubbish assistant referee who loves to interfere by sticking his flag up for offside every two minutes!

G **...is for GINGER DUDES!**
Everybody loves ginger footballers! Their funny orange hair looks mega cool on the green pitch!

H **...is for HOMER SIMPSON!**
The Simpsons star is the celebrity cartoon look-alike of Aston Villa striker Marlon Harewood!

L **...is for LOADED!**
The old dudes around the world who are buying Premier League teams are mega rich – they're 'loaded'!

M **...is for MAMMOTH!**
A team which is miles behind the league leaders face a 'mammoth task' to catch them! It basically means big!

N **...is for NO-NONSENSE!**
It's the perfect way to describe big defenders who love roughing up strikers!

FOOTBALL!

U **...is for UNFASHIONABLE!**
A club famous for never winning anything is often called 'unfashionable'!

V **...is for VAN!**
Holland's top stars always seem to be named after those big white vehicles – like Van Persie, Van Nistelrooy, Van der Sar and Van der Vaart!

W **...is for WAGS!**
Stands for 'Wives And Girlfriends'! Top footballers, however ugly, always have a fit missus!

Y **...is for Y-FRONTS**
If you want to make it as a pro, you can't be wearing these! You'll be the butt of all the dressing room jokes!

X **...is for X-RATED!**
When things get heated, watch out for the horror tackles flying in!

Z **...is for ZIDANE!**
The world's best player between 1998 and 2004! But all he's remembered for is THAT crazy headbutt!

SUPER MARLON!

Aston Villa striker Marlon Harewood says his favourite computer game is Super Mario Kart!

I'd beat you, MATCH!

DEANO ♥ DIGESTIVES!

West Ham striker Dean Ashton thinks eating biscuits the night before a game brings him luck!

KINGS OF ENGLAND!

THE TWO MOST SUCCESSFUL TEAMS IN ENGLAND ARE MAN. UNITED AND LIVERPOOL, BUT WHICH CLUB HAS WON MORE TROPHIES?

MAN. UNITED		LIVERPOOL
2	CHAMPIONS LEAGUE	5
0	UEFA CUP	3
16	LEAGUE TITLE	18
11	FA CUP	7
2	LEAGUE CUP	7
31	TOTAL	40

HA, HA! YOU'VE NEVER WON THE PREM!

THE REDS ROCK!

RONALDO'S FAVE DOG!

Christmas comes early for AC Milan's chunky striker Ronaldo...

Get off my hot dogs, boss!

★ 2007

ARSENAL
WOULD BE...
EMINEM

Five years ago they couldn't stop winning things, but they haven't been the same force over the last couple of seasons!

ASTON VILLA
WOULD BE...
GREEN DAY

They've been knocking around the top ten for years, but nobody gets very excited by them any more – except their hardcore fans!

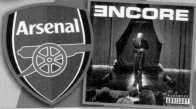

DERBY
WOULD BE...
MIKA

It's been an amazing 12 months for them, but you'd be surprised if they're still doing the business this time next year!

EVERTON
WOULD BE...
U2

They've got a huge fan base and they're usually near the top, but they haven't been all that succesful since the 1980s!

FULHAM
WOULD BE...
PRINCE

Used to be good years and years ago, but now they never make an impression at the top! You can't knock them for effort, though!

LIVERPOOL
WOULD BE...
ABBA

Awesome in the 1970s and 1980s and still do really well in Europe, but they haven't been No.1 in England for years!

PORTSMOUTH
WOULD BE...
JUSTIN TIMBERLAKE

They've performed consistently over the last couple of years, but some people still aren't too sure whether they like them or not!

READING
WOULD BE...
LILY ALLEN

Burst on to the scene last year and made everyone sit up and take notice! It'll be difficult to keep up that form this year, though!

Michael Owen has worn the No.10 shirt at every club he's played for – apart from Real Madrid! He had the No.11 for them!

GEORGE'S WHEELS!

George Boateng drives a blinged-up Porsche Cayenne Turbo!

IT'S WELL FAST!

BIRMINGHAM
WOULD BE...
DIZZEE RASCAL
Every couple of years they'll do something totally awesome, but in between you're never quite convinced by them!

BLACKBURN
WOULD BE...
OASIS
They're from the North West and rocked in the mid-90s, but they've struggled to hit those heights ever since!

BOLTON
WOULD BE...
DESTINY'S CHILD
After losing their leader, people are wondering if they can survive or whether we've seen the last of them!

CHELSEA
WOULD BE...
KANYE WEST
They're mega rich, think they're the best thing ever and have been well successful over the last three years!

IF FOOTY CLUBS WERE... POP STARS!!

Premier League clubs and popstars have got more in common than you think...

MAN. CITY
WOULD BE...
THE SPICE GIRLS
They're back after years of doing nothing! They've got loads of money and they're ready to hit the big-time again!

MAN. UNITED
WOULD BE...
MADONNA
Loved by millions and hated by everyone else! They're totally loaded and always put on a spectacular show!

MIDDLESBROUGH
WOULD BE...
BLACK EYED PEAS!
There was lots of hype about them two years ago, but after losing their star performer things aren't looking too good any more!

NEWCASTLE
WOULD BE...
ELTON JOHN
They've got an army of fans all over the world, but they've not done anything decent for a very, very long time!

SUNDERLAND
WOULD BE...
TAKE THAT
They're back in business after a while out of the spotlight, but the big question is how long can they stay there?

TOTTENHAM
WOULD BE...
ARCTIC MONKEYS
Great things are expected of these exciting youngsters after two years of knocking on the door of the big-time!

WEST HAM
WOULD BE...
BRITNEY SPEARS
After a successful couple of years, people thought they were finished! But they survived and are now on the way back!

WIGAN
WOULD BE...
SHAYNE WARD
Two years ago was as good as it was ever going to get for them! Can they survive this year, or will they completely disappear?

DADDY'S BOY!

Jose Mourinho's Dad used to play in goal for Portugal!

Catch it, old man!

"YEAH, BABY!"

Wayne Rooney's favourite film is Austin Powers!

It's ace!

GOAL KINGS!

Who were the top scorers in Europe's top leagues last season? MATCH finds out...

ENGLAND PREMIER LEAGUE
DIDIER DROGBA
Chelsea ★ 20 goals

FRANCE LIGUE 1
PAULETA
PSG ★ 15 goals

SPAIN LA LIGA
RUUD VAN NISTELROOY
Real Madrid ★ 25 goals

SCOTLAND PREMIER LEAGUE
KRIS BOYD
Rangers ★ 20 goals

ITALY SERIE A
FRANCESCO TOTTI
Roma ★ 26 goals

GERMANY BUNDESLIGA
THEOFANIS GEKAS
Bochum ★ 20 goals!

PREM M£

SUPER TORRES IS ROLLING IN IT!

FERNANDO TORRES
LIVERPOOL STRIKER
23 years old
£90,000

I'M WORTH IT, MATCH!

RIO FERDINAND
MAN. UNITED DEFENDER
28 years old
£100,000

I CAN BUY NUFF HAIR GEL NOW!

WAYNE ROONEY
MAN. UNITED STRIKER
21 years old
£110,000

CRISTIANO RONALDO
MAN. UNITED WINGER
22 years old
£119,000

ANDRIY SHEVCHENKO
CHELSEA STRIKER
31 years old
£121,000

FRANK LAMPARD
CHELSEA MIDFIELDER
29 years old
£100,000

REAL'S RABBIT!

Wicked Real Madrid striker Javier Saviola is nicknamed 'El Conejo' – which means 'The Rabbit' in Spanish!

Got any carrots?

ST. JAMES' RECORD!

Newcastle's record home attendance is 68,386! It was against Chelsea way back in 1930!

GA BUCK$!

Footy stars are loaded – but who gets the most? Here's the Prem's top earners and their rumoured weekly wage!

MICHAEL OWEN
NEWCASTLE STRIKER
27 years old
£110,000

LI'L MO'S A WELL BIG EARNER, DUDES!

STEVEN GERRARD
LIVERPOOL MIDFIELDER
27 years old
£120,000

YA! I'M ROLLING IN IT!

MICHAEL BALLACK
CHELSEA MIDFIELDER
31 years old
£131,000

JOHN TERRY
CHELSEA DEFENDER
26 years old
£131,000

DAVID BECKHAM... E-MAILS HOME!

MATCH has had a peek at the e-mails Becks might have been sending to his mate Gaz Neville... err, maybe!

To: gary.neville@man.united.com
Subject: The USA

Gaz,
I've got a new friend over here in the USA. His name is Mickey. His voice is even squeakier than mine – and his ears are bigger than Rooney's! He's got a cool girlfriend too – she's called Minnie. Victoria loves her spotty dress! Becks xxx

To: gary.neville@man.united.com
Subject: The USA

Neviller,
Here's a photo Minnie took of me and Mickey! I got him a trial with the Galaxy – but he got a bit confused and thought it was American Football! Bless him!
Becks xxx

To: gary.neville@man.united.com
Subject: The USA

G-Man,
I've attached a pic of Mickey and Minnie. I took it when they came to watch me play for the Galaxy! Mickey got kicked out in the second half coz he was shouting too much at the ref!
Becks xxx

DID YOU KNOW?
WICKED STARS CRISTIANO RONALDO AND STEVEN GERRARD HAVE BEEN NAMED IN THE PFA PREMIER LEAGUE TEAM OF THE SEASON FOR THE LAST TWO YEARS IN A ROW!

WE RULE!

HISTORY LESSON!
BEFORE 1992, GOALKEEPERS WERE ALLOWED TO PICK UP BACK-PASSES!

SPFC

2001
He makes his first team debut for Sao Paulo!

1982
Little Kaka is born in Brasilia - the capital of Brazil!

1990
Brazilian giants Sao Paulo snap him up when he's only eight years old!

THE WICKED STORY OF...
KAKA!

2003
Milan A.C.
Italian giants AC Milan splash out £4.5 million to bring Kaka to Europe!

2002
Scouts from Europe's biggest clubs fly to Brazil to watch him play, as he hits nine goals in just 22 games!

2002
His awesome club form means he's called up to the Brazil squad - and he makes his debut against South American rivals Bolivia!

the champions league IN NUMBERS!

9
REAL MADRID HAVE WON THE CHAMPIONS LEAGUE AN AMAZING NINE TIMES! IT'S A RECORD!

2

THE NUMBER OF TIMES THE FINAL OF THE COMPETITION HAS INVOLVED TWO TEAMS FROM THE SAME COUNTRY!

4

IS HOW MANY ENGLISH CLUBS HAVE WON IT - VILLA, LIVERPOOL, MAN. UNITED & NOTTINGHAM FOREST!

1967

THE YEAR CELTIC WON THE TOURNAMENT! THEY'RE THE ONLY SCOTTISH TEAM TO HAVE LIFTED THE TROPHY!

YOUR NUMBER'S UP!

AC MILAN WILL STOP USING THE NO.3 SHIRT WHEN PAOLO MALDINI HANGS UP HIS BOOTS! BUT IF ANY OF HIS CHILDREN PLAY FOR THE CLUB, THEY'LL BE ALLOWED TO WEAR IT!

he said wot?

"We are like the primary school boys walking into the secondary school for the first time and finding out who the bullies are!"

Derby boss Billy Davies on life in the Premier League!

2004

Kaka averages a goal every three games in his first season at the San Siro, helping Milan win the Serie A title and the European Super Cup!

2005

Kaka is voted the Champions League's best midfielder as Milan storm to the final before losing to Liverpool on penalties!

I'M THE BEST PLAYER IN THE WORLD, DUDES!

2006

Footy experts reckon Kaka will be the star of the World Cup - but things don't go to plan as Brazil crash out in the quarter-finals!

2007

He goes goal-crazy in the Champo League, smashing in ten goals to finish as the top scorer as Milan win the trophy!

MATCH LOOKS BACK AT THE CLASSY CAREER OF AC MILAN AND BRAZIL STAR KAKA!

FACTFILE!

Full Name: Ricardo Izecson dos Santos Leite
Age: 25
Position: Midfielder
Club: AC Milan
Shirt Number: 22
Country: Brazil

2008?

Real Madrid have been chasing him for yonks, and newspaper reports reckon they're prepared to pay way more than £50 million for him!

3 THE NUMBER OF CLUBS AC MILAN ACE CLARENCE SEEDORF HAS WON THE CHAMPO LEAGUE WITH!

10 ARSENAL'S MEGA DEFENCE KEPT TEN CLEAN SHEETS IN A ROW IN THE 2005-06 TOURNAMENT!

5 THE NUMBER OF PLAYERS WHO SCORED A HAT-TRICK ON THEIR CHAMPIONS LEAGUE DEBUT!

40 THAT'S HOW OLD ALESSANDRO COSTACURTA WAS WHEN HE PLAYED FOR AC MILAN LAST SEASON!

YOU AIN'T AS GOOD AS ME, PAL!

ROBBIE & RON!

You da man, Keano!

Tottenham's Robbie Keane was team-mates with Brazil striker Ronaldo at Inter Milan in 2001!

CAUGHT ON C

World's best player!

MP3 player!

WAKE UP, LOSERS!

Ronaldinho loves his two best mates – but they can't stop sleeping!

Check out what the mega MATCH cameras have spotted!

Kaka loves Stevie G so much that he even prays at his feet!

YOU'VE GOT THAT RIGHT!

I'M NOT WORTHY, STEVIE!

Pray maker!

Play maker!

Oldest fan in the world?

CALL 999, DUDE!

AAAGH!

Has this German footy star been picked off by a sniper? That's harsh!

FOOTY ACROBATS!

NANI
MAN. UNITED

10 /10

OBAFEMI MARTINS
NEWCASTLE

5 /10

MICAH RICHARDS
MAN. CITY

2 /10

ROBBIE KEANE
TOTTENHAM

5 /10

SUPER STADIUMS!
The biggest footy stadiums in the UK…

WEMBLEY
England ★ 90,000

OLD TRAFFORD
Man. United ★ 76,212

MILLENNIUM STADIUM
Wales ★ 74,500

CELTIC PARK
Celtic ★ 60,832

EMIRATES STADIUM
Arsenal ★ 60,432

AMERA!

Ivan Campo?

Carlos Puyol?

CAN'T CATCH ME!

GIVE US A CHANCE, BECKS!

Who said life would be well easy for Becks in the MLS?

I'LL TAKE THAT!

Sammy Eto'o!

Sonny Eto'o!

With Eto'o distracted by a fan, Thierry Henry nicks his son's pocket money!

THESE DUDES ALL LOVE TO CELEBRATE IN SPECTACULAR STYLE – BUT WHO'S THE BEST?

ROBERT EARNSHAW
DERBY

8 /10

JULIUS AGHAHOWA
WIGAN

9 /10

GUESS WHO!
Which footy superstar do these boots belong to?

Answer: David Beckham.

TORRES ROCKS!

Rock this!

LIVERPOOL STRIKER FERNANDO TORRES HAS REVEALED HE'D BE A ROCK STAR IF HE WASN'T A FOOTBALLER! THAT'S AWESOME!

DID YOU KNOW...?
LIVERPOOL ARE THE ONLY CLUB IN THE TOP FLIGHT WHO HAVE HAD THE SAME SHIRT SPONSOR SINCE THE PREM STARTED BACK IN 1992!

TATTOO CRAZY!

How cool is 'tat'?
Tottenham midfielder Kevin-Prince Boateng has 13 tattoos!

WHO ARE YA?

Take the big **MATCH** test to find out which footy star you're most like...

You wanna be JT, dudes!

No way, Terry!

Big Ron rocks!

Q1
YOU'RE IN THE DRESSING ROOM BEFORE THE MATCH. WHAT ARE YOU DOING?
- A. Shouting and getting everyone going! ✓
- B. Doing your hair in front of the mirror! ✓
- C. Praying to God! ✓
- D. Stuffing your face with cake! ✓

Q2
YOU RECEIVE THE BALL EARLY IN THE GAME. WHAT DO YOU DO?
- A. Play a simple pass to a team-mate!
- B. Do a couple of stepovers!
- C. Go forward and play an inch-perfect pass! ✓
- D. Stop and think about half-time hot dogs! ✓

Q3
A ROCK-SOLID MIDFIELDER IS CHARGING TOWARDS YOU. WHAT DO YOU DO?
- A. Go crunching in on him!
- B. Get your team's hardest player to stop him!
- C. Use your speed to get to the ball first! ✓
- D. Forget it and eat a crispy pancake!

Q4
YOUR TEAM WINS A FREE-KICK ON THE EDGE OF THE AREA. WHAT WILL YOU DO?
- A. Try to get on the end of the cross! ✓
- B. Go for a powerful shot at goal! ✓
- C. Catch the 'keeper out with a quick shot! ✓
- D. Use the delay to leg it to the buffet! ✓

Q5
YOU'VE JUST SCORED A LAST-MINUTE WINNER. HOW DO YOU CELEBRATE?
- A. Quickly sprint back into position! ✓ ✓
- B. Go crazy and run to the crowd!
- C. Thank God for helping you out! ✓
- D. Phone the local takeaway for a pizza! ✓

Q6
IT'S SUNDAY MORNING AND YOU'RE CHILLING OUT. WHAT DO YOU WATCH ON TV?
- A. Match Of The Day! You love it! ✓
- B. Hollyoaks! The girls are gorgeous! ✓
- C. Songs Of Praise – and you sing along! ✓
- D. TV? You're too busy making breakfast! ✓

MOSTLY A'S!
You are JOHN TERRY! You'd make a wicked captain coz you're well tough, mega brave and a real leader!
THAT'S ME! ✓

MOSTLY B'S!
You are CRISTIANO RONALDO! You love the way you look, you've got the skills and you're a crowd pleaser!
THAT'S ME! ✓

MOSTLY C'S!
You are KAKA! You're a silky-skilled star who scores and creates goals – and you're a big fan of God, too!
THAT'S ME! ✓

MOSTLY D'S!
You are RONALDO! You're not a bad player and you can still score goals – but you love your food!
THAT'S ME! ✓

MATCH!

CHAMPO LEAGUE STARS!

RUUD VAN NISTELROOY

FACT FILE!

CLUB: Real Madrid

POSITION: Striker **AGE:** 31

TROPHY COUNT – 8:
2 Eredivisie, 2 Dutch Super Cup, 1 Premiership, 1 La Liga, 1 FA Cup & 1 League Cup.

BOOTS:
Nike Tiempo Legend.

CHAMPO LEAGUE FACT:
The lethal Dutch striker holds the record for the most Champo League goals in one season – 12 for Man. United in 2003!

WORLD'S GREATEST TEAM!

MATCH *has been on a mega scouting mission to create the greatest team on the planet!*
Check out which stars made our dream starting XI, then pick your own fave line-up!

GOALKEEPERS!

IN MATCH'S TEAM!

IKER CASILLAS

REAL MADRID ★ AGE: 26 ★ SPAIN

TRANSFER VALUE: £14 MILLION

Real fans love Casillas! He played his first game when he was just 18 and has won the Champions League twice. His saves and reflexes are awesome!

PETR CECH

CHELSEA ★ AGE: 25 ★ CZECH REP.

TRANSFER VALUE: £20 MILLION

Most footy fans and experts reckon Cech is the best goalkeeper in the world! The Chelsea hero makes amazing saves, brave blocks and cool catches – it takes something special to beat Big Pete!

GIANLUIGI BUFFON

JUVENTUS ★ AGE: 29 ★ ITALY

TRANSFER VALUE: £18 MILLION

Buffon cost Juventus a world record £32.6 million in 2001! He's won stacks of trophies for his club and helped Italy win the World Cup in 2006!

PEPE REINA

LIVERPOOL ★ AGE: 25 ★ SPAIN

TRANSFER VALUE: £12 MILLION

Reina joined The Reds in 2005 and soon proved why he's world class! The Spain international is the best in the business at saving penalties!

SANTIAGO CANIZARES

VALENCIA ★ AGE: 37 ★ SPAIN

TRANSFER VALUE: £2 MILLION

He's an old dude now, but Canizares is still class! The ex-Real Madrid star has won four La Liga titles, the Champions League and the UEFA Cup! Legend!

MATCH'S TOP FIVE!

1. PETR CECH
2. GIANLUIGI BUFFON
3. IKER CASILLAS
4. PEPE REINA
5. SANTIAGO CANIZARES

I'M PICKING...

1.

WORLD'S GREATEST TEAM!

FULL-BACKS!

IN MATCH'S TEAM!

DANIEL ALVES

SEVILLA ★ AGE: 24 ★ BRAZIL

TRANSFER VALUE: £24 MILLION

The tricky Brazil ace plays more like a winger than a full-back! He's always bombing forward to join in with attacks and whip in some wicked crosses!

WAYNE BRIDGE

CHELSEA ★ AGE: 27 ★ ENGLAND

TRANSFER VALUE: £8 MILLION

Bridgey's quick, tough in the tackle and his crossing is top notch! A player with his skill should be playing every week, not sitting on the bench!

GIANLUCA ZAMBROTTA

BARCELONA ★ AGE: 30 ★ ITALY

TRANSFER VALUE: £16 MILLION

Zambrotta is a world-class full-back! He plays on the right for Barcelona but he's just as good at left-back! The Italy star has also got a lethal shot and he's not afraid to have a pop at goal!

PHILIPP LAHM

BAYERN MUNICH ★ AGE: 23 ★ GERMANY

TRANSFER VALUE: £14 MILLION

Lahm is a winger's nightmare! He's got tons of pace, he's strong and he can use both feet, so he's ultra-tough to get past! He's also great going forward!

ERIC ABIDAL

BARCELONA ★ AGE: 28 ★ FRANCE

TRANSFER VALUE: £8 MILLION

Barça bagged themselves a top-class talent when they signed Eric Abidal from Lyon last summer! He's solid at the back and supports his wingers too!

IN MATCH'S TEAM!

GARY NEVILLE
MAN. UNITED ★ AGE: 32 ★ ENGLAND
TRANSFER VALUE: £6 MILLION
The Man. United captain is a defending machine! He never lets his team down at the back, and he loves overlapping Ronaldo when The Red Devils attack!

ASHLEY COLE
CHELSEA ★ AGE: 26 ★ ENGLAND
TRANSFER VALUE: £20 MILLION
Ash is one of the fastest defenders on Earth! There's nothing he loves more than overtaking a flying winger to make a tackle, then bombing forward and getting a great cross in! He's a speed machine!

MIGUEL
VALENCIA ★ AGE: 27 ★ PORTUGAL
TRANSFER VALUE: £10 MILLION
Miguel has been La Liga's best right-back since joining Valencia two years ago. He's got loads of skill and he scores some cracking goals!

MAREK JANKULOVSKI
AC MILAN ★ AGE: 30 ★ CZECH REP.
TRANSFER VALUE: £8 MILLION
The Czech powerhouse has replaced AC Milan legend Paolo Maldini at left-back and looks totally unbeatable! He's a key player for the Euro champs!

JAVIER ZANETTI
INTER MILAN ★ AGE: 34 ★ ARGENTINA
TRANSFER VALUE: £3 MILLION
The Inter and Argentina right-back has been marking wingers out of games for years! Zanetti is the ultimate attacking full-back – his dribbling is amazing!

MATCH'S TOP TEN!

1	GIANLUCA ZAMBROTTA
2	ASHLEY COLE
3	ERIC ABIDAL
4	PHILIPP LAHM
5	MAREK JANKULOVSKI
6	MIGUEL
7	GARY NEVILLE
8	DANIEL ALVES
9	JAVIER ZANETTI
10	WAYNE BRIDGE

I'M PICKING...

1	....
2	....

RAUL'S RIVAL PAST!

Legendary Real Madrid goal machine **Raul** started his career at massive city rivals Atletico Madrid!

Shhh, MATCH!

DID YOU KNOW...?

THERE ARE MORE FRENCH PLAYERS IN THE PREM THAN IN ANY OTHER WORLD LEAGUE – APART FROM FRANCE!

THE NEXT BIG THING!

CARDIFF's CHRIS GUNTER is one of the hottest young talents in the game! MATCH meets the teenager with the footy world at his feet!

MEGA FACT!
The classy defender made his full Wales debut in a friendly against New Zealand last summer!

MEGA FACT!
The wicked wonderkid made his Cardiff debut in the Carling Cup last season! He was just 17 at the time!

Gunter is a top right-back who bombs forward to join attacks! He's got bags of pace and skill!

CHRIS GUNTER!

CLUB: Cardiff
AGE: 18
POSITION: Right-back
TRANSFER VALUE: £3.5 million
TOP SKILL: Sprinting forward to support attacks!

Gunter shares a room with ace Tottenham left-back Gareth Bale when he's on Wales duty!

INTERNATIONAL RECORD:

WALES UNDER-15: Caps: 4 Goals: 0
WALES UNDER-16: Caps: 4 Goals: 0
WALES UNDER-17: Caps: 11 Goals: 2
WALES UNDER-19: Caps: 3 Goals: 0
WALES UNDER-21: Caps: 3 Goals: 0
FULL WALES: Caps: 1 Goals: 0

MEGA FACT!
Chris is a massive Cardiff fan and used to go to watch them play before he signed as a pro with The Bluebirds!

MEGA FACT!
The full-back was so good last season that he was named Championship Apprentice Of The Year!

CHRIS ON...

...HIS STRENGTHS!
"I love to attack when we've got the ball! I've become faster as I've got older and my passing is quite good! I really love going forward!"

...TRANSFER TALK!
"It's a confidence boost to see my name linked with top Premier League teams, but Cardiff is the club I've always supported!"

...WALES CAPS!
"Winning my first cap for Wales was brilliant! I didn't expect to get picked but I ended up starting the match against New Zealand, which was absolutely fantastic!"

...HIS HERO!
"That's probably Gary Neville – I've never seen a winger get the better of him! His long throws and crossing are great!"

...HIS FUTURE!
"Hopefully – if things go the way they are planned to with Cardiff – I will be in the Premier League with this club and we'll be doing really well at our brand-new stadium!"

MATCH!

CHAMPO LEAGUE STARS!

FACT FILE!

CLUB: Liverpool

POSITION: Midfielder **AGE:** 27

TROPHY COUNT – 7:
2 FA Cup, 2 League Cup,
1 Champions League, 1 UEFA
Cup & 1 European Super Cup.

BOOTS:
Adidas +Predator Absolute.

CHAMPO LEAGUE FACT:
The Liverpool ace went to bed
with the Champo League trophy
the night they won it in 2005!

STEVEN GERRARD

CENTRE-BACKS!

FABIO CANNAVARO

REAL MADRID ★ AGE: 33 ★ ITALY

TRANSFER VALUE: £10 MILLION

Fab's getting on a bit now, but he still seems to get better every season! He's quick, strong and hardly ever loses a header – even though he's well tiny!

JOHN TERRY

IN MATCH'S TEAM!

CHELSEA ★ AGE: 26 ★ ENGLAND

TRANSFER VALUE: £30 MILLION

Chelsea and England captain JT is the best centre-back in the world by miles! He'll do anything to stop the opposition from scoring, and he even pops up with match-winning headers at the other end!

ALESSANDRO NESTA

AC MILAN ★ AGE: 31 ★ ITALY

TRANSFER VALUE: £12 MILLION

Nesta has been putting strikers in his pocket for years! He's always in the right place at the right time, ready to crunch whoever's got the ball!

RIO FERDINAND

MAN. UNITED ★ AGE: 28 ★ ENGLAND

TRANSFER VALUE: £20 MILLION

Rio's got everything a top defender needs – he's quick, strong, comfortable on the ball, good in the air and always in the right position! What a legend!

CARLOS PUYOL

BARCELONA ★ AGE: 29 ★ SPAIN

TRANSFER VALUE: £20 MILLION

Barça legend Puyol looks a bit crazy thanks to his daft mop-top, but don't let that fool you – he's a solid centre-back who loves bossing strikers!

SERGIO RAMOS

REAL MADRID ★ AGE: 21 ★ SPAIN

TRANSFER VALUE: £25 MILLION

Ramos has been rockin' for Real Madrid and Spain! He can play in the centre or on the right and doesn't fear anyone! He's still well young too!

KOLO TOURE

ARSENAL ★ AGE: 26 ★ IVORY COAST

TRANSFER VALUE: £20 MILLION

Even if a striker gets past Kolo, the big Arsenal star almost always catches them up and nabs the ball back thanks to his rocket-powered speed!

IN MATCH'S TEAM!

RAFAEL MARQUEZ

BARCELONA ★ AGE: 28 ★ MEXICO

TRANSFER VALUE: £14 MILLION

Rafa's a total footballer – he loves having the ball and controlling games! He can also mix it with the biggest and best strikers when he needs to!

JAMIE CARRAGHER

LIVERPOOL ★ AGE: 29 ★ ENGLAND

TRANSFER VALUE: £20 MILLION

Like England team-mate John Terry, Carragher throws himself in front of everything to protect his goal! JC isn't the quickest, but even the world's fastest strikers find it tough to get past him!

NEMANJA VIDIC

MAN. UNITED ★ AGE: 26 ★ SERBIA

TRANSFER VALUE: £16 MILLION

No-one knew anything about Vidic before Fergie brought him to United last year, but now the super-strong cruncher is one of the best!

MATCH'S TOP TEN!

1. JOHN TERRY
2. JAMIE CARRAGHER
3. FABIO CANNAVARO
4. ALESSANDRO NESTA
5. CARLOS PUYOL
6. NEMANJA VIDIC
7. RAFAEL MARQUEZ
8. RIO FERDINAND
9. SERGIO RAMOS
10. KOLO TOURE

I'M PICKING...

1. ....
2. ....

WORLD'S GREATEST TEAM!

CENTRAL MIDFIELDERS!

IN MATCH'S TEAM!

MICHAEL ESSIEN
CHELSEA ★ AGE: 24 ★ GHANA
TRANSFER VALUE: £25 MILLION

Essien is the ultimate midfield machine! He wears the opposition down with his powerful running, and will play anywhere on the pitch to help his team!

STEVEN GERRARD
LIVERPOOL ★ AGE: 27 ★ ENGLAND
TRANSFER VALUE: £50 MILLION

Stevie G runs the show for Liverpool AND England! He won't stop running until his team's winning – which means he'll be tackling back on the edge of his box one minute, then bagging a winner!

FRANK LAMPARD
CHELSEA ★ AGE: 29 ★ ENGLAND
TRANSFER VALUE: £30 MILLION

For pure goalscoring, no midfielder can get anywhere near Franky Lamps! He lets his pals do the tackling so he can concentrate on hitting screamers!

ANDREA PIRLO
AC MILAN ★ AGE: 28 ★ ITALY
TRANSFER VALUE: £30 MILLION

Milan and Italy legend Pirlo is such a clever player that he always has time on the ball. He's a master creator who also whips in lethal free-kicks!

CESC FABREGAS
ARSENAL ★ AGE: 20 ★ SPAIN
TRANSFER VALUE: £35 MILLION

Every team in the world would love to have Cesc bossing their midfield! Arsenal would be lost without his perfect passing and tough tackling!

JUAN RIQUELME

VILLARREAL ★ AGE: 29 ★ ARGENTINA

TRANSFER VALUE: £15 MILLION

Riquelme gets loads of stick for not tracking back, but he makes up for it when he's got he ball! His top through-balls and ace free-kicks are wicked!

IN MATCH'S TEAM!

KAKA

AC MILAN ★ AGE: 25 ★ BRAZIL

TRANSFER VALUE: £50 MILLION

Kaka can unlock any defence thanks to his amazing dribbling and pinpoint passing! He can do whatever he wants with the ball at his feet, and he's got the skills to dance through and score!

DIEGO

WERDER BREMEN ★ AGE: 22 ★ BRAZIL

TRANSFER VALUE: £20 MILLION

Diego's played so well for Werder that he's now a key man for Brazil! The ball sticks to him like glue and his passing is more accurate than Sat Nav!

PAUL SCHOLES

MAN. UNITED ★ AGE: 32 ★ ENGLAND

TRANSFER VALUE: £6 MILLION

The Man. United genius proved last season that he's still one of the best playmakers in world footy! If only he'd come back to play for England!

XABI ALONSO

LIVERPOOL ★ AGE: 25 ★ SPAIN

TRANSFER VALUE: £20 MILLION

Stevie G is the main man for Liverpool, but Alonso is the unsung hero! He's always there when his team-mates need him – and he chips in with goals!

MATCH'S TOP TEN!

1	KAKA
2	STEVEN GERRARD
3	CESC FABREGAS
4	MICHAEL ESSIEN
5	ANDREA PIRLO
6	FRANK LAMPARD
7	DIEGO
8	XABI ALONSO
9	JUAN RIQUELME
10	PAUL SCHOLES

I'M PICKING...

1	
2	

MATCH SPY!

Georgios Samaras gets tons of stick from his Man City team-mates for listening to dodgy 1980s music!

SHOLA'S MUST-HAVES!

Newcastle striker Shola Ameobi says the three things he always takes with him on away trips are a toothbrush, a DVD player and... moisturising cream!

MATCHY's got his hands on a magic crystal ball! Take a look at what he predicts for 2008...

MYSTIC MATCHY!

APRIL

Chelsea take on Man. United at The Bridge and a bad tackle by Essien sends Fergie wild! The United boss climbs on the dugout and does an elbow drop on Jose!

Bring it on, Jose!

FEBRUARY

Ronaldinho gets his teeth fixed, but it turns out to be a bad move – scientists discover that all his awesome football powers were coming from his teeth! He quits footy and starts work as a bin man!

This stinks, MATCH!

MAY

Arsene Wenger's decision to play his young stars backfires on the last day of the Premier League season! The Gunners are winning 1-0 when they suddenly run off to watch the new series of Tracy Beaker!

Get back here!

AUGUST

Man. City boss Sven buys an Orang-utan to make his sandwiches! But an injury crisis on Manchester derby day forces Sven to play 'Orangy' up front! He bags a wicked hat-trick!

Thomas Cook.com

OCTOBER

ENGLAND

Grrr!

There are crazy scenes at Wembley! Stuart Pearce is watching his England Under-21 team struggle against Macedonia. He runs on to the pitch and gets so angry that he explodes!

DECEMBER

A spaceship sucks Newcastle manager Sam Allardyce up! A week later, millions of alien Big Sams fall to Earth from outer space! They slime everyone with their lasers and take over the world!

CHAMPO LEAGUE STARS!

FACT FILE!

CLUB: Roma

POSITION: Forward **AGE:** 31

TROPHY COUNT – 2: 1 Serie A & 1 Coppa Italia.

BOOTS: Diadora Maximus.

CHAMPO LEAGUE FACT: The tricky hitman scored four goals in nine Champions League games last season before Roma were dumped out by a red-hot Man. United!

FRANCESCO TOTTI

WINGERS!

IN MATCH'S TEAM!

ROBINHO

REAL MADRID ★ AGE: 23 ★ BRAZIL

TRANSFER VALUE: £20 MILLION

Speedster Robinho has so many tricks, you get a headache just watching him! He won his first La Liga title in 2007 and wants more glory this season!

RONALDINHO

BARCELONA ★ AGE: 27 ★ BRAZIL

TRANSFER VALUE: £40 MILLION

The Samba star has twice been crowned FIFA's World Player Of The Year! Ronnie busts out mind-blowing tricks and blasts in wonder goals for Barça and Brazil! MATCH loves his goofy grin, too!

FRANCK RIBERY

BAYERN MUNICH ★ AGE: 24 ★ FRANCE

TRANSFER VALUE: £18 MILLION

Ribery is a fiery winger who drives at defenders before setting up goals or blasting rocket shots into the net! He's gonna be a Bayern legend!

RYAN GIGGS

MAN. UNITED ★ AGE: 33 ★ WALES

TRANSFER VALUE: £3.5 MILLION

Giggsy has been ripping it up for United since he was 17 years old! The ancient winger loves dancing down the wing and making defenders look daft!

DEJAN STANKOVIC

INTER MILAN ★ AGE: 29 ★ SERBIA

TRANSFER VALUE: £10 MILLION

Stankovic scored six goals last season as Inter won the title! He's got a rocket shot, and fans love him because he gives 100 per cent in every game!

SIMAO

ATLETICO MADRID ★ AGE: 27 ★ PORTUGAL

TRANSFER VALUE: £14 MILLION

Simao is such a class player that he can play anywhere in midfield! He's awesome at cutting in from the wing and unloading long-range screamers!

CRISTIANO RONALDO

MAN. UNITED ★ AGE: 22 ★ PORTUGAL

TRANSFER VALUE: £40 MILLION

Rockin' Ronaldo was the best player in the Prem last season! The United ace is lightning-quick and the ball sticks to his feet like glue! He loves doing stepovers, so getting the ball off him is a nightmare!

DAVID SILVA

VALENCIA ★ AGE: 21 ★ SPAIN

TRANSFER VALUE: £12 MILLION

Loads of top clubs are sniffing around Silva! The Spain wizard is becoming a huge star in La Liga because of his deadly left foot and clever footy brain!

LIONEL MESSI

BARCELONA ★ AGE: 20 ★ ARGENTINA

TRANSFER VALUE: £38 MILLION

Messi is one of the hottest youngsters in world footy! He's quality on the left wing for Barça and is a massive danger when he darts inside and goes for goal!

JOE COLE

CHELSEA ★ AGE: 25 ★ ENGLAND

TRANSFER VALUE: £15 MILLION

Tricky England star Joe Cole can do anything with the ball! He can dribble, pass, shoot, pull out tricks, bend in free-kicks and score crucial goals!

MATCH'S TOP TEN!

1. RONALDINHO
2. CRISTIANO RONALDO
3. LIONEL MESSI
4. ROBINHO
5. DEJAN STANKOVIC
6. SIMAO
7. JOE COLE
8. FRANCK RIBERY
9. RYAN GIGGS
10. DAVID SILVA

I'M PICKING...

1 ....
2 ....

WORLD'S GREATEST TEAM!

STRIKERS!

IN MATCH'S TEAM!

DIMITAR BERBATOV

TOTTENHAM ★ AGE: 26 ★ BULGARIA

TRANSFER VALUE: £26 MILLION

Berba hit 23 goals in all competitions last season and helped Spurs finish fifth in the Prem! He's got a great first touch and is lethal around the box!

DIDIER DROGBA

CHELSEA ★ AGE: 29 ★ IVORY COAST

TRANSFER VALUE: £25 MILLION

Chelsea's powerful predator is the kind of striker every defender hates to face! He slams home volleys from 30 yards, buries power headers and speeds away from centre-backs with his mega pace!

RUUD VAN NISTELROOY

REAL MADRID ★ AGE: 31 ★ HOLLAND

TRANSFER VALUE: £12 MILLION

Fergie thought Ruud was finished when he forced him out of Old Trafford, but the deadly Dutchman proved his class by leading Real to the title in 2006-07!

SAMUEL ETO'O

BARCELONA ★ AGE: 26 ★ CAMEROON

TRANSFER VALUE: £30 MILLION

If you give Sammy an inch of space he'll destroy you! The Cameroon ace is quick, clever and never stops working. He's a crucial player for Barcelona!

WAYNE ROONEY

MAN. UNITED ★ AGE: 21 ★ ENGLAND

TRANSFER VALUE: £35 MILLION

The young United hitman is one of the most feared strikers on Earth! He makes loads of chances for his team and scores some wicked screamers!

DAVID VILLA

VALENCIA ★ AGE: 25 ★ SPAIN

TRANSFER VALUE: £32 MILLION

The Valencia hero gives defenders nightmares with his clever movement, lightning pace and deadly finishing! He loves bagging long-range screamers!

CARLOS TEVEZ

MAN. UNITED ★ AGE: 23 ★ ARGENTINA

TRANSFER VALUE: £26 MILLION

The Argentina megastar can win footy matches all on his own! His silky skills, awesome energy, amazing vision and bullet shots are world-class weapons!

IN MATCH'S TEAM!

MIROSLAV KLOSE

BAYERN MUNICH ★ AGE: 29 ★ GERMANY

TRANSFER VALUE: £15 MILLION

The Germany international is great in the air and ice-cool in front of goal! He was the top scorer at World Cup 2006 and is a Bundesliga legend!

THIERRY HENRY

BARCELONA ★ AGE: 30 ★ FRANCE

TRANSFER VALUE: £20 MILLION

Barcelona bagged themselves a bargain when they signed Henry from Arsenal last summer! The flash France striker creates chances out of nothing and burns away from defenders with his electric pace!

FRANCESCO TOTTI

ROMA ★ AGE: 31 ★ ITALY

TRANSFER VALUE: £10 MILLION

Totti was pure class in Serie A last season! He went totally goal crazy for Roma and picked up the European Golden Boot after netting 26 times!

MATCH'S TOP TEN!

1	THIERRY HENRY
2	DIDIER DROGBA
3	WAYNE ROONEY
4	SAMUEL ETO'O
5	DAVID VILLA
6	RUUD VAN NISTELROOY
7	DIMITAR BERBATOV
8	MIROSLAV KLOSE
9	CARLOS TEVEZ
10	FRANCESCO TOTTI

I'M PICKING...

1	....
2	....

WORLD'S GREATEST TEAM!

MATCH'S TEAM!

CHECK OUT MATCH'S ACE TEAM!

CECH

ZAMBROTTA

TERRY

CARRAGHER

COLE

RONALDO

GERRARD

KAKA

RONALDINHO

DROGBA

HENRY

NOW FILL IN YOUR FAVE PLAYERS!

GOALKEEPER
....

RIGHT-BACK
....

CENTRE-BACK
....

CENTRE-BACK
....

LEFT-BACK
....

RIGHT-WING
....

CENTRAL MIDFIELD
....

CENTRAL MIDFIELD
....

LEFT-WING
....

STRIKER
....

STRIKER
....

CHAMPO LEAGUE STARS!

FACT FILE!

CLUB: Inter Milan

POSITION: Striker **AGE:** 32

TROPHY COUNT – 11:
3 Argentina Premier League,
3 Italian Super Cup, 1 UEFA
Cup, 1 Premier League,
1 Serie A, 1 Copa Libertadores
& 1 Coppa Italia.

BOOTS:
Adidas +Predator Absolute.

CHAMPO LEAGUE FACT:
Crespo scored twice in the 2005
Champo League final for AC
against Liverpool – but still lost!

HERNAN CRESPO

LA LIGA QUIZ!

How much do you know about Spanish footy? Answer these ten brain-busters to get maximo points!

1

Which La Liga club play their home games at the Mestalla Stadium?
....

2

Who is the manager of Real Madrid?
....

3

Which club did Diego Forlan sign for last summer?
....

4

Which club has won more La Liga titles - Athletic Bilbao or Sevilla?
....

5

Name this 'keeper with funky hair!
....

6

True or False? Barcelona legend Ronaldinho used to play for French side PSG.
....

7

Which class La Liga club won the UEFA Cup last season?
....

8

Which national team does mega Atletico Madrid midfielder Maniche play for?
....

9

Which of these Prem stars hasn't played for Real Madrid - Michael Owen, Jonathan Woodgate or Andriy Shevchenko?
....

10

Which slick Spanish team play in this cool home kit?
....

MY SCORE /10

ANSWERS ON PAGE 92!

MATCH!

CHAMPO LEAGUE STARS!

DIDIER DROGBA

FACT FILE!

CLUB: Chelsea

POSITION: Striker **AGE:** 29

TROPHY COUNT – 5:
2 Premier League, 2 League Cup & 1 FA Cup.

BOOTS:
Nike Mercurial Vapor III.

CHAMPO LEAGUE FACT:
Drogba became the first Blues player to score a Champions League hat-trick with his treble against Levski Sofia in 2006!

EURO 2008

HERE WE COME!

The European Championships are gonna rock next summer, so check out MATCH's wicked guide to the class tournament!

© 2004 UEFA TM

MEGA TOURNAMENT!

The top 16 footy countries in Europe can't wait to battle it out for the title! Big teams like Brazil and Argentina can't play in the Euros, but there will still be loads of awesome players in action!

GROUPING UP!

There will be four groups at Euro 2008, each packed with four wicked European countries! Only the top two from each group will reach the knockout stages, so it's well tough from the start!

BIG EURO DATES!

GROUP STAGES	June 7-18
QUARTER-FINALS	June 19-22
SEMI-FINALS	June 25-26
FINAL	June 29

MENTAL MASCOTS!

This pair of jokers will be the dudes to know next summer! Trix and Flix are the official Euro 2008 mascots, so they'll probably be messing around on the pitch at all the matches!

TURN OVER FOR MORE EURO 2008 STUFF!

THE HOSTS!

FAB FACT!
Austria could be the lowest-ranked team at the finals!

WALS-SIEZENHEIM
SALZBURG

CAPACITY: 30,000

TIVOLI NEU STADIUM
INNSBRUCK

CAPACITY: 30,000

• Linz
• Wels
Upper Austria
Steyr •
• Salzburg
Salzburg
Voralberg
• Feldkirch
Tirol
• Bludenz
Landeck
Tirol
Lienz •
Carinthia
Villach •
• Klagenfurt

FAB FACT!
Switzerland have never got past the group stages!

ST. JAKOB-PARK
BASLE

CAPACITY: 42,500

Euro 2008 kicks off here on June 7!

WANKDORF STADIUM
BERNE

CAPACITY: 32,000

Basel
• Zurich
• Bern

GENEVA STADIUM
GENEVA

CAPACITY: 30,000

Geneva

CHAMPO LEAGUE STARS!

FACT FILE!

CLUB: Man. United

POSITION: Midfielder **AGE:** 22

TROPHY COUNT – 3:
1 Premier League, 1 FA Cup & 1 League Cup.

BOOTS:
Nike Mercurial Vapor III.

CHAMPO LEAGUE FACT:
Ronnie scored his first-ever Champo League goals when he bagged twice in the 7-1 quarter-final whupping of Roma!

CRISTIANO RONALDO

PATRICK VIEIRA...
MY CLASS

1995 MILAN MOVER!

PATRICK SAYS: "It was a massive move, because Cannes are a small club and AC Milan are huge! Going into the dressing room and seeing players like Maldini, Baresi, Savicevic, Boban and Weah was fantastic!"

1994 CANNES CAPTAIN!

PATRICK SAYS: "It was great for me to come into the team so young! Cannes had one of the best youth systems around, and it was a terrific time for my career because I worked under a great manager who helped me!"

1998 WORLD CUP WINNER!

PATRICK SAYS: "The 1998 World Cup victory was really good! I didn't play quite as much as I did in other international tournaments, but it was still a World Cup winners' medal and I will treasure it forever!"

1998 AWESOME ARSENAL!

PATRICK SAYS: "I had so many great moments at Arsenal that it's hard to choose highlights! Winning the first Double in 1998 was great, but so was claiming the title at Man. United and Tottenham, our two main rivals!"

2000 EURO STAR!

PATRICK SAYS: "Euro 2000 was different, because I played in every game and it felt like I'd really won it! I also think France can do really well in the next few years because we have some great young players in the squad!"

CAREER!

INTER MILAN legend **PATRICK VIEIRA** talks **MATCH** through the top moments of his career!

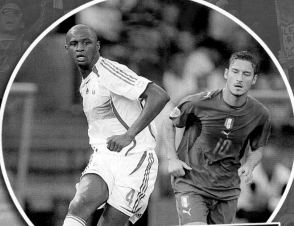

2007 SERIE A STAR!

PATRICK SAYS: "I came to Inter Milan because I wanted to win more trophies! I had a great first season at the club, when we won Serie A, and I would love to lift the Champions League trophy as an Inter player!"

2006 WORLD CUP WONDER!

PATRICK SAYS: "World Cup 2006 was a great experience! It wasn't quite fantastic, because to win it would have been fantastic. We couldn't quite make the final step, but we were happy to get as far as we did!"

2005 JUVE GOTTA LOVE IT!

PATRICK SAYS: "I loved my time with Juventus! I came to Italy because I wanted to experience the Italian league! I didn't think I needed to prove that I was a good player – I'd already done that at Arsenal!"

VIEIRA'S TROPHY TRACKER!

Check out all the mega trophies Vieira has won during his career!

CLUB FOOTY	
FA CUP	4
PREMIER LEAGUE	3
SERIE A	1
ITALIAN SUPER CUP	1

TOTAL 11

INTERNATIONAL FOOTY	
WORLD CUP	1
EURO CHAMPIONSHIP	1

SERIE A QUIZ!

Tackle these ten teasers to show how much you know about Italian footy! Bet you can't get full points!

1
Which Roma ace was Serie A's top scorer last season?
....

2
WINNER
CHAMPIONS LEAGUE 2007
How many times have AC Milan won the Champions League?
....

3
Which Italian team play in this girly kit?
....

4
Name this wicked Inter Milan and Brazil goal machine!
....

5
Which ex-Chelsea manager is now the boss of Juventus?
....

6
True or False? Juventus shot-stopper Gianluigi Buffon is the most expensive 'keeper ever.
....

7
What is AC Milan striker Ronaldo's crazy squad number - 77, 88 or 99?
....

8
Which team has won more Serie A titles - Fiorentina or Sampdoria?
....

9
Which country does Roma defender Philippe Mexes play for?
....

10
Inter and AC Milan share this stadium, but what is it called?
....

MY SCORE /10

ANSWERS ON PAGE 92!

MATCH!

FACT FILE!

CLUB: Barcelona

POSITION: Striker **AGE:** 30

TROPHY COUNT – 7:
3 FA Cup, 2 Premier League,
1 Ligue 1 & 1 French Super Cup.

BOOTS: Reebok Sprintfit.

CHAMPO LEAGUE FACT:
Henry became Arsenal's all-time
top scorer with his goal in the
Champions League against
Sparta Prague back in 2005! It
was his 186th for The Gunners!

THIERRY HENRY

TOP SECRET!

TOP SECRET

MATCH brings you all the hottest rumours, gossip and secrets from the wicked world of football!

1 Brazil striker **Ronaldo** used to keep big tortoises in his garden when he played for Real Madrid! The tubby goal machine let them splash around in his swimming pool!

2 Ace Chelsea skipper **John Terry** is mega superstitious! The England hero always sits in the same seat on the team bus and has worn the same pair of shinpads for more than ten years!

3 Awesome Liverpool striker **Fernando Torres** once starred in a cheesy music video in Spain! Well rubbish pop band 'El Canto del Loco' used 'El Nino' as the main character in their vid!

4 Middlesbrough's **Emmanuel Pogatetz** loves Britain so much that he has a Union Jack painted on the top of his cool Mini Cooper! What a total legend!

5 Bayern Munich and France star **Franck Ribery** is wicked at playing the saxophone! The France trickster learned how to play the weird-looking instrument when he was just 12 years old!

6 Cardiff striker **Robbie Fowler** partied with Real Madrid on their open-top bus after they won the Spanish title back in 2003! His best mate Steve McManaman was playing for Real at the time!

7 Flying Fulham midfielder **Clint Dempsey** isn't just a top-class footballer – he's also a big-time rap star in the USA! Dempsey calls himself 'Deuce' and busts out loads of slick tunes!

8 Mega eco-warrior **David James** has converted his car so it runs on rapeseed oil instead of petrol! The Pompey 'keeper wants to be more environmentally friendly! Nice one, Jamo!

10 Deadly AC Milan and Italy striker **Pippo Inzaghi** is a qualified accountant! He'd be an ace person to have around if you get bored doing all your rubbish maths homework!

9 Rushden & Diamonds star **Curtis Woodhouse** was also a professional boxer! Big Curtis knocked out his first opponent back in 2006, so don't mess with him!

TOP SECRET!

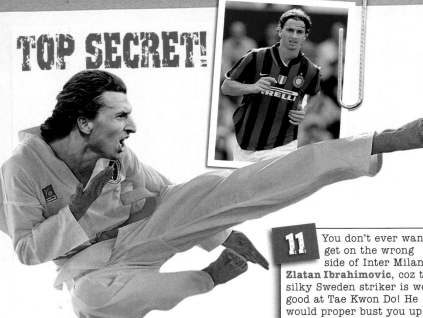

11 You don't ever wanna get on the wrong side of Inter Milan's **Zlatan Ibrahimovic**, coz the silky Sweden striker is well good at Tae Kwon Do! He would proper bust you up!

12 Man. United trickster **Carlos Tevez** is the lead singer of a rock band called 'Piola Vago' in Argentina! The band released their first album back in 2005! Rock on, Carlos!

13 Giant striker **Peter Crouch** almost didn't become a footy player! Crouchy was awesome at tennis when he was younger and reckons he could have been a pro!

14 Pompey hero **Sol Campbell** became a top movie star when he played the part of a mega-tough bouncer in 1990s British film 'Snatch'! No-one messes with big Sol!

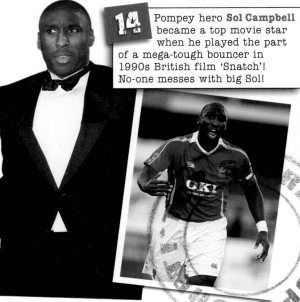

15 **Dimitar Berbatov** says he learned to speak English by watching loads of gangster films! Berba checked out the movies before he joined Spurs back in 2006!

16 **Sir Alex Ferguson** once signed striker **Diego Forlan** for Man. United even though he'd never seen him play! Fergie had only watched the hitman on video!

17 Crazy Fulham defender **Moritz Volz** rides his folding bike to all of The Cottagers' home games instead of travelling on the team bus! Get in there, Volzy!

18 **Wayne Rooney** can't get to sleep unless there's loads of noise in his bedroom! The Man. United hitman turns a hoover or hairdryer on before he goes to bed!

19 **Jose Mourinho** had a run-in with the police last season when they tried to take his dog away! The cops wanted to put Jose's pooch into quarantine!

20 Real Madrid defender **Sergio Ramos** is a huge fan of bull fighting! The classy Spain centre-back says he always wanted to be a matador when he was younger!

21 Roma skipper **Francesco Totti** nearly signed for AC Milan when he was younger, but his Mum wouldn't let him go! She said young Francesco had to play his footy in Rome!

TOP SECRET!

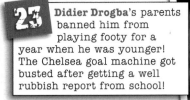

22 England Under-21 left-back **Leighton Baines** is learning to play the guitar! Bainesy is teaching himself because he's too embarrassed to have proper lessons!

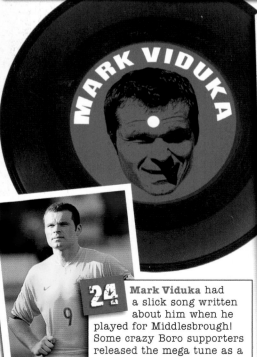

25 England star **Rio Ferdinand** once injured himself trying to pick up his TV remote! The Man. United defender damaged tendons in his knee and was ruled out of action for ages!

24 **Mark Viduka** had a slick song written about him when he played for Middlesbrough! Some crazy Boro supporters released the mega tune as a download single last season!

27 Fulham's **Jimmy Bullard** could play for Germany at Euro 2008! Jimmy was born in England, but he qualifies for the German national team because his Gran is from there!

26 West Ham winger **Nolberto Solano** loves playing the trumpet and has even set up his own salsa band called 'The Geordie Latinos'! Is Nobby cool or what?

28 Real Madrid striker **Ruud van Nistelrooy** started his career as an awesome defender! Can you imagine Ruud playing alongside Cannavaro in the centre of Real's defence?

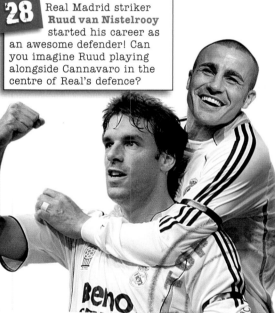

30 Man. City's **Rolando Bianchi** had a total nightmare on his first day with the club! His taxi driver dropped him off at the United training ground by accident!

29

Tottenham and England striker **Jermain Defoe** really hates going swimming! JD makes his girlfriend check how deep every swimming pool is before he goes near the water!

MATCH ANNUAL 2008! 55

SPOT THE STARS!

There are ten ace Championship stars hiding in this mega footy crowd! Spot them all to net full points!

MY SCORE /10

ANSWERS ON PAGE 92!

MATCH!

CHAMPO LEAGUE STARS!

CESC FABREGAS

FACT FILE!

CLUB: Arsenal

POSITION: Midfielder **AGE:** 20

TROPHY COUNT – 1:
1 FA Cup.

BOOTS: Nike Tiempo Legend.

CHAMPO LEAGUE FACT:
Fabregas had only just turned
19 when he played for Arsenal
in the 2006 Champions League
Final against Barcelona! The
Gunners lost the match 2-1!

PREM SUPER

20

LEICESTER

SEASONS IN PREM: 8
HIGHEST FINISH! 8th (2000)
BIGGEST WIN! 4-0 v Leeds, 2003
BIGGEST DEFEAT! 1-6 v Arsenal, 2000
PREM GOAL KING! Emile Heskey
PREM HERO! Muzzy Izzet

FAB FACT! The Foxes finished in the top ten of the Premier League four seasons on the trot from 1997 to 2000!

19

CHARLTON

SEASONS IN PREM: 8
HIGHEST FINISH! 7th (2004)
BIGGEST WIN! 5-0 v Southampton, 1998
BIGGEST DEFEAT! 1-6 v Leeds, 2003
PREM GOAL KING! Darren Bent
PREM HERO! Chris Powell

FAB FACT! Charlton were scrapping for a Champo League spot in 2003-04, but just missed out after a poor finish!

18

BOLTON

SEASONS IN PREM: 8
HIGHEST FINISH! 6th (2005)
BIGGEST WIN! 5-0 v Leicester, 2001
BIGGEST DEFEAT! 0-6 v Man. United, 1996
PREM GOAL KING! Kevin Davies
PREM HERO! Kevin Nolan

FAB FACT! Bolton totally hammered Leicester 5-0 in their first away game of the season back in 2001-02!

17

WIMBLEDON

SEASONS IN PREM: 8
HIGHEST FINISH! 6th (1994)
BIGGEST WIN! 5-0 v Watford, 1999
BIGGEST DEFEAT! 1-7 v Aston Villa, 1995
PREM GOAL KING! Dean Holdsworth
PREM HERO! Robbie Earle

FAB FACT! Wimbledon is what MK Dons were called when they played in the Prem! They changed their name in 2004!

LEAGUE!

Who is the Premier League's best ever team? MATCH added up every team's Prem results since it began in 1992 to find out!

16

SHEFFIELD WEDNESDAY

SEASONS IN PREM: 8
HIGHEST FINISH! 7th (1993, 1994 & 1997)
BIGGEST WIN: 5-0 v West Ham, 1993
BIGGEST DEFEAT: 0-8 v Newcastle, 1999
PREM GOAL KING! Mark Bright
PREM HERO! Des Walker

FAB FACT! Wednesday finished the first Prem season in 7th place and reached the FA Cup and League Cup finals!

15

COVENTRY

SEASONS IN PREM: 9
HIGHEST FINISH! 11th (1994 & 1998)
BIGGEST WIN: 5-0 v Blackburn, 1995
BIGGEST DEFEAT! 1-6 v Chelsea, 2000
PREM GOAL KING! Dion Dublin
PREM HERO: Richard Shaw

FAB FACT! When Coventry were relegated in 2001, it ended an amazing spell of 34 years in the top division!

14

MAN. CITY

SEASONS IN PREM: 10
HIGHEST FINISH! 8th (2005)
BIGGEST WIN: 5-0 v Everton, 2000
BIGGEST DEFEAT! 0-6 v Liverpool, 1995
PREM GOAL KING! Niall Quinn
PREM HERO! Shaun Goater

FAB FACT! City were relegated from the Premier League in 1996, and just two seasons later went down to League 1!

13

MIDDLESBROUGH

SEASONS IN PREM: 12
HIGHEST FINISH! 7th (2005)
BIGGEST WIN! 6-1 v Derby, 1997
BIGGEST DEFEAT! 0-7 v Arsenal, 2006
GOAL KING! Yakubu
PREM HERO! Juninho

FAB FACT! Boro were docked three points in 1997 coz they cancelled a fixture at Blackburn! It meant they got relegated!

PREM SUPER LEAGUE!

12

SOUTHAMPTON

SEASONS IN PREM: 13
HIGHEST FINISH! 8th (2003)
BIGGEST WIN! 5-1 v Swindon, 1993
BIGGEST DEFEAT! 1-7 v Liverpool, 1999
GOAL KING! Matt Le Tissier
PREM HERO! Matt Le Tissier

FAB FACT! Southampton had been playing in the top flight for 27 years before they eventually went down in 2005!

11

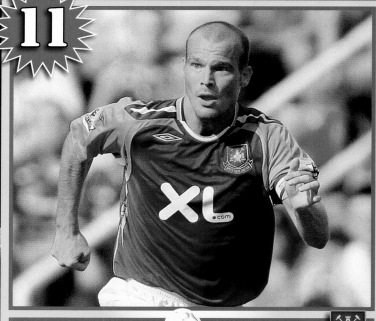

WEST HAM

SEASONS IN PREM: 12
HIGHEST FINISH! 5th (1999)
BIGGEST WIN! 6-0 v Barnsley, 1998
BIGGEST DEFEAT! 1-7 v Man. United, 2000
GOAL KING! Paolo di Canio
PREM HERO Julian Dicks

FAB FACT! West Ham reached the FA Cup final at the end of their first season back in the top flight in 2005-06!

10

LEEDS

SEASONS IN PREM: 12
HIGHEST FINISH! 3rd (2000)
BIGGEST WIN! 6-1 v Bradford, 2001
BIGGEST DEFEAT! 1-6 v Portsmouth, 2003
GOAL KING! Mark Viduka
PREM HERO! Gary Kelly

FAB FACT! Leeds reached the semi-finals of the Champions League in 2001, but were relegated just three years later!

9

EVERTON

SEASONS IN PREM: 15
HIGHEST FINISH! 4th (2005)
BIGGEST WIN! 7-1 v Southampton, 1996
BIGGEST DEFEAT! 0-7 v Arsenal, 2005
GOAL KING! Kevin Campbell
PREM HERO! Duncan Ferguson

FAB FACT! The Toffees finished fourth in 2005 to reach the Champo League, but crashed out in the qualifying stages!

8

7

BLACKBURN

SEASONS IN PREM: 13
PREM TITLES! 1
BIGGEST WIN! 7-0 v Nottingham Forest, 1995
BIGGEST DEFEAT! 0-5 v Coventry, 1995
GOAL KING! Alan Shearer
PREM HERO! Tim Sherwood

FAB FACT! Blackburn won the Prem title in 1995 just three years after getting promoted! Get in there, Rovers!

TOTTENHAM

SEASONS IN PREM: 15
HIGHEST FINISH: 5th (2006 & 2007)
BIGGEST WIN! 7-2 v Southampton, 2000
BIGGEST DEFEAT! 1-7 v Newcastle, 1996
GOAL KING! Teddy Sheringham
PREM HERO! David Ginola

FAB FACT! Spurs have only finished above North London rivals Arsenal twice in the Prem – in 1993 and 1995!

6

5

ASTON VILLA

SEASONS IN PREM: 15
HIGHEST FINISH! 2nd (1993)
BIGGEST WIN! 7-1 v Wimbledon, 1995
BIGGEST DEFEAT! 0-5 v Arsenal, 2006
GOAL KING! Dwight Yorke
PREM HERO! Paul McGrath

FAB FACT! Villa nearly won the first ever Premier League title back in 1993 after topping the table for most of the season!

NEWCASTLE

SEASONS IN PREM: 14
HIGHEST FINISH! 2nd (1996 & 1997)
BIGGEST WIN! 8-0 v Sheffield Wednesday, 1999
BIGGEST DEFEAT! 0-5 v Chelsea, 2003
GOAL KING! Alan Shearer
PREM HERO! Alan Shearer

FAB FACT! Newcastle had a 12-point lead over Man. United at the top of the Prem in 1996 but blew it and finished second!

PREM SUPER LEAGUE!

4

3

LIVERPOOL

SEASONS IN PREM: 15
HIGHEST FINISH! 2nd (2002)
BIGGEST WIN! 7-1 v Southampton, 1999
BIGGEST DEFEAT! 1-5 v Coventry, 1992
GOAL KING! Robbie Fowler
PREM HERO! Steven Gerrard

FAB FACT! Robbie Fowler scored the fastest Prem hat-trick in four minutes 32 seconds against Arsenal back in 1994!

CHELSEA

SEASONS IN PREM: 15
PREM TITLES! 2
BIGGEST WIN! 6-0 v Barnsley, 1997
BIGGEST DEFEAT! 1-5 v Liverpool, 1996
GOAL KING! Jimmy Floyd Hasselbaink
PREM HERO: John Terry

FAB FACT! The Blues won the league title for the first time in 50 years in 2005, and then lifted the trophy again in 2006!

2

ARSENAL

SEASONS IN PREM: 15
PREM TITLES! 3
BIGGEST WIN! 7-0 v Middlesbrough, 2006
BIGGEST DEFEAT! 1-6 v Man. United, 2001
GOAL KING! Thierry Henry
PREM HERO! Patrick Vieira

FAB FACT! Arsenal went 49 league games unbeaten between 2003 and 2004. The wicked run spread over three seasons!

MAN. UNITED

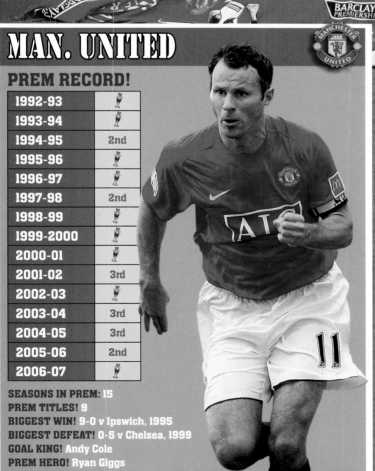

PREM RECORD!

1992-93	🏆
1993-94	🏆
1994-95	2nd
1995-96	🏆
1996-97	🏆
1997-98	2nd
1998-99	🏆
1999-2000	🏆
2000-01	🏆
2001-02	3rd
2002-03	🏆
2003-04	3rd
2004-05	3rd
2005-06	2nd
2006-07	🏆

SEASONS IN PREM: 15
PREM TITLES! 9
BIGGEST WIN! 9-0 v Ipswich, 1995
BIGGEST DEFEAT! 0-5 v Chelsea, 1999
GOAL KING! Andy Cole
PREM HERO! Ryan Giggs

FAB FACT! United won the Premier League title, the FA Cup and the Champions League all in one season back in 1999!

OVERALL TABLE

		P	W	D	L	F	A	PTS
1.	Man. United	582	367	131	84	1140	516	1232
2.	Arsenal	582	308	157	117	974	516	1081
3.	Chelsea	582	285	158	139	912	580	1013
4.	Liverpool	582	285	144	153	925	579	999
5.	Newcastle	540	229	142	169	799	653	829
6.	Aston Villa	582	214	175	193	711	673	817
7.	Tottenham	582	212	152	218	773	786	788
8.	Blackburn	506	205	132	169	702	607	747
9.	Everton	582	192	159	231	703	775	735
10.	Leeds	468	189	125	154	641	573	692
11.	West Ham	464	160	116	188	549	649	596
12.	Southampton	506	150	137	219	598	738	587
13.	Middlesbrough	460	143	133	184	550	631	559
14.	Man. City	392	114	110	168	442	526	452
15.	Coventry	354	99	112	143	387	490	409
16.	Sheff. Wed.	316	101	89	126	409	453	392
17.	Wimbledon	316	99	94	123	384	472	391
18.	Bolton	304	97	85	122	358	438	378
19.	Charlton	304	93	82	129	342	442	361
20.	Leicester	308	84	90	134	354	456	342

Stats correct up to the start of the 2007-08 season!

BUNDESLIGA QUIZ!

The German league is class, but how much do you know about it? See if you can pick up all ten points!

1

Which massive club won the Bundesliga title last season?

....

2

Which country does Werder Bremen striker Markus Rosenberg play for?

....

3

Name this mega famous Bundesliga stadium!

....

4

Which ace German team wear this home kit?

....

5

Holland midfield hero Rafael Van der Vaart plays for which awesome Bundesliga club?

....

6

Which giant Italy striker signed for Bayern Munich last summer?

....

7

Where did Schalke finish in last year's Bundesliga table?

....

8

At which club's ground did England play their opening match of the 2006 World Cup - was it Wolfsburg or Eintracht Frankfurt?

....

9

True or False? Bayer Leverkusen have never won the German title.

....

10

Which Prem club did Stuttgart ace Thomas Hitzlsperger once play for?

....

BAYERN MÜNCHEN

MY SCORE /10

ANSWERS ON PAGE 92!

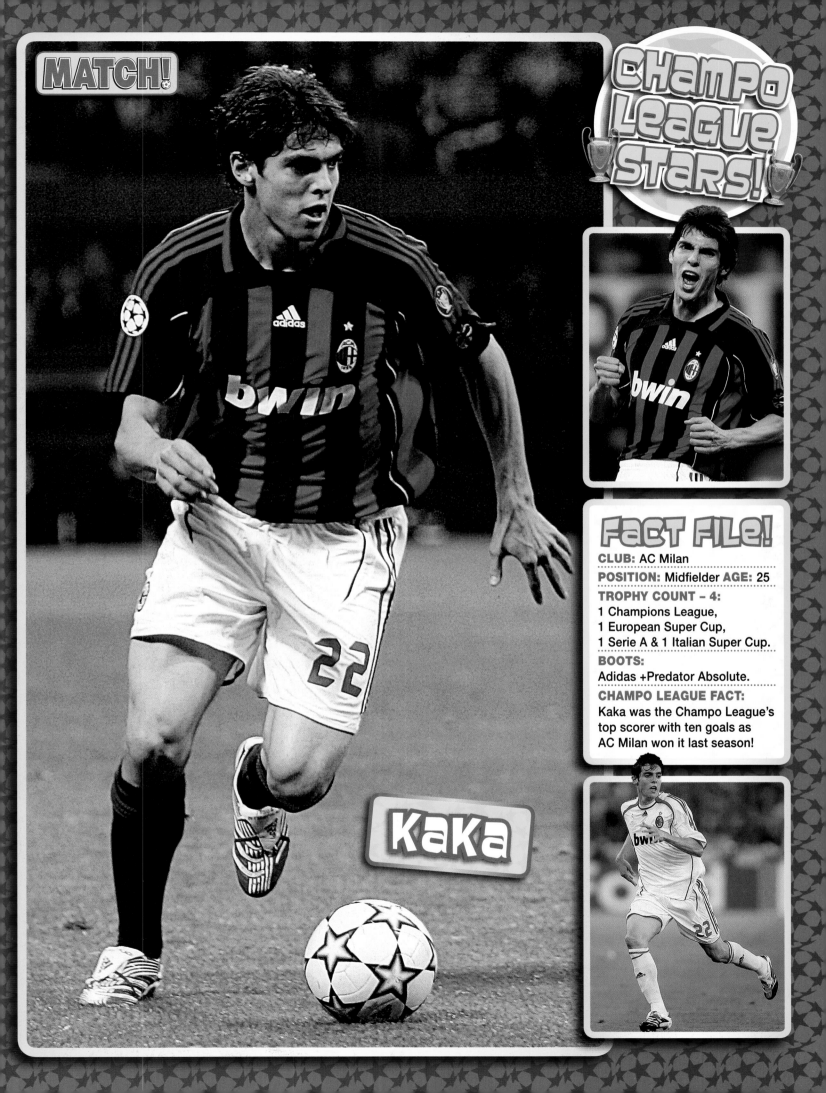

MATCH!

CHAMPO LEAGUE STARS!

FACT FILE!

CLUB: AC Milan

POSITION: Midfielder **AGE:** 25

TROPHY COUNT – 4:
1 Champions League,
1 European Super Cup,
1 Serie A & 1 Italian Super Cup.

BOOTS:
Adidas +Predator Absolute.

CHAMPO LEAGUE FACT:
Kaka was the Champo League's
top scorer with ten goals as
AC Milan won it last season!

Kaka

THE WORLD'S...
BIGGEST GAMES!

MATCH goes all over the planet to bring you the world's hottest footy fixtures!

BARCELONA v REAL MADRID

STADIUM
Nou Camp - 98,600

YEAR FORMED
1899

NICKNAME
Blaugranes
(The Blue-Maroons)

GAFFER
Frank Rijkaard

LEAGUE TITLES
16

STAR MEN
Ronaldinho, Thierry Henry,
Lionel Messi

MEGA MATCH RATING! 8

STADIUM
The Bernabeu - 80,000

YEAR FORMED
1902

NICKNAME
Los Merengues
(The Meringues)

GAFFER
Bernd Schuster

LEAGUE TITLES
30

STAR MEN
Ruud van Nistelrooy,
Raul, Wesley Sneijder

THE HISTORY

'El Classico' is much more than a meeting of Spain's top two teams - Barça want to be independent from the rest of the country! Top players like Luis Figo and Ronaldo have moved from Barça to Real in recent years and have been pelted with pig's heads. Mingin'!

W	D	L	HEAD TO HEAD	W	D	L
58	30	66		66	30	58

CELTIC v RANGERS

STADIUM
Celtic Park - 60,832

YEAR FORMED
1888

NICKNAME
The Bhoys

GAFFER
Gordon Strachan

LEAGUE TITLES
41

STAR MEN
Shunsuke Nakamura,
Artur Boruc, Aiden McGeady

STADIUM
Ibrox - 50,444

YEAR FORMED
1873

NICKNAME
The Gers

GAFFER
Walter Smith

LEAGUE TITLES
51

STAR MEN
Barry Ferguson,
Kris Boyd, Daniel Cousin

THE HISTORY
Rangers and Celtic's rivalry goes way beyond footy! It's all about religion, so the two teams have hated each other ever since they were formed! Celtic have been the top team in recent years but Rangers have won more titles, so these games are always well tasty!

W	D	L		HEAD TO HEAD		W	D	L
92	82	110				110	82	92

ROMA v LAZIO

STADIUM
Stadio Olimpico - 82,000

YEAR FORMED
1927

NICKNAME
Giallorossi
(The Yellow-Reds)

GAFFER
Luciano Spalletti

LEAGUE TITLES
3

STAR MEN
Francesco Totti,
Daniele de Rossi, Mancini

STADIUM
Stadio Olimpico - 82,000

YEAR FORMED
1900

NICKNAME
Biancocelesti
(White & Sky Blue)

GAFFER
Delio Rossi

LEAGUE TITLES
2

STAR MEN
Luciano Zauri, Stefano
Mauri, Daniel Ledesma

THE HISTORY
AC Milan against Inter is the flashest Italian derby, but this one's the real grudge match! They have to share the Stadio Olimpico, and Roma fans hate the fact Lazio's fans are from the posh part of the city! The crowd goes crazy when the Rome derby kicks off!

W	D	L		HEAD TO HEAD		W	D	L
50	50	37				37	50	50

BOCA JUNIORS v RIVER PLATE

MEGA MATCH 9 RATING!

STADIUM
La Bombonera - 57,400

YEAR FORMED
1905

NICKNAME
Los Xeneizes
(People Of Genoa)

GAFFER
Miguel Russo

LEAGUE TITLES
23

STAR MEN
Martin Palermo, Rodrigo
Palacio, Ever Banega

STADIUM
El Monumental - 65,645

YEAR FORMED
1901

NICKNAME
Los Millonarios
(The Millionaires)

GAFFER
Daniel Passarella

LEAGUE TITLES
32

STAR MEN
Fernando Belluschi, Mauro
Rosales, Leonardo Ponzio

THE HISTORY
These two teams have ruled Argentinian footy
for 70 years! Boca are the people's club, while
River Plate are known as The Millionaires!
Boca fans call River 'Gallinas', or chickens,
while River say Boca are 'Los Puercos', or
pigs, coz they reckon their stadium stinks!

W	D	L		HEAD TO HEAD		W	D	L
65	55	60				60	55	65

INTER MILAN v AC MILAN

MEGA MATCH 7 RATING!

STADIUM
San Siro - 85,700

YEAR FORMED
1908

NICKNAME
Nerazzurri
(The Black-Blues)

GAFFER
Roberto Mancini

LEAGUE TITLES
15

STAR MEN
Dejan Stankovic, Zlatan
Ibrahimovic, Christian Chivu

STADIUM
San Siro - 85,700

YEAR FORMED
1899

NICKNAME
Rossoneri
(The Red-Blacks)

GAFFER
Carlo Ancelotti

LEAGUE TITLES
17

STAR MEN
Kaka, Andrea Pirlo,
Gennaro Gattuso

THE HISTORY
This is the most famous derby in Italian footy!
Inter were formed by a mix of Italian and
international players who were sick of AC's
success with an all-Italian team! Since then
they've matched each other for trophies,
which makes these mega games extra spicy!

W	D	L		HEAD TO HEAD		W	D	L
60	52	56				56	52	60

LIVERPOOL v MAN. UNITED

STADIUM
Anfield - 45,362

YEAR FORMED
1892

NICKNAME
The Reds

GAFFER
Rafael Benitez

LEAGUE TITLES
18

STAR MEN
Steven Gerrard, Jamie Carragher, Fernando Torres

STADIUM
Old Trafford - 76,212

YEAR FORMED
1878

NICKNAME
The Red Devils

GAFFER
Sir Alex Ferguson

LEAGUE TITLES
16

STAR MEN
Wayne Rooney, Cristiano Ronaldo, Ryan Giggs

MEGA MATCH 8 RATING!

THE HISTORY
These two teams are the most successful in England, and always want to beat the other! United have won more in recent years, but Liverpool ruled in the 70s and 80s! They hate each other so much that Alex Ferguson even refused to sell Gabriel Heinze to The Reds!

W	D	L		HEAD TO HEAD		W	D	L
49	43	56				56	43	49

FENERBAHCE v GALATASARAY

STADIUM
Sukru Saracoglu - 50,509

YEAR FORMED
1907

NICKNAME
Sari Kanaryalar (Yellow Canaries)

GAFFER
Zico

LEAGUE TITLES
17

STAR MEN
Stephen Appiah, Roberto Carlos, Mateja Kezman

STADIUM
Ali Sami Yen - 23,785

YEAR FORMED
1905

NICKNAME
Aslanlar (The Lions)

GAFFER
Karl-Heinz Feldkamp

LEAGUE TITLES
16

STAR MEN
Hakan Sukur, Lincoln, Hasan Sas

MEGA MATCH 9 RATING!

THE HISTORY
There's always fireworks when these two play! Fenerbahce and Galatasaray are both from Istanbul, but Gala is in Europe while Fener is in Asia! Galatasaray laugh at Fenerbahce for being rubbish in Europe, but Fener fans love the fact they've won loads more derby games!

W	D	L		HEAD TO HEAD		W	D	L
39	30	30				30	30	39

THE STARS'... TOP FOOTY

PAUL ROBINSON
TOTTENHAM ★ GOALKEEPER

ROBBO SAYS:
"The best tip I can think of is to work hard and always try to improve your game! Try to play as much football as you can and never let anyone tell you that you can't do it! You need to believe in yourself!"

JAMIE CARRAGHER
LIVERPOOL ★ CENTRE-BACK

JAMIE SAYS:
"The most important thing is to be the best player you can be. Everybody has different levels of skill, but you have to make the most of what you've got and be the best player you can possibly be!"

ARJEN ROBBEN
REAL MADRID ★ WINGER

ARJEN SAYS:
"Just enjoy your football! See how far you go in the game, but enjoy it. Of course, if you really want it, you have to work hard. But you have to enjoy football, and if you're talented it will come!"

ASHLEY YOUNG
ASTON VILLA ★ WINGER

ASHLEY SAYS:
"You've got to have dedication! You need passion and desire, and have to know what you want to get out of the game! It's important to be the one player in your team that stands out from the rest of the lads!"

TIPS!

OBAFEMI MARTINS
NEWCASTLE ★ STRIKER

OBAFEMI SAYS:
"You need to be yourself! You must be honest with yourself, remember who you are and believe in what you can do. As long as you work hard and keep doing your best, then you will succeed!"

GAEL CLICHY
ARSENAL ★ LEFT-BACK

GAEL SAYS:
"Consistency is very important! Watch as many games as you can, then try to copy the best players like Ronaldinho, Ronaldo and Thierry Henry. But you can learn from any player, so you should just watch games and learn!"

RYAN GIGGS
MAN. UNITED ★ WINGER

RYAN SAYS:
"If you want to make it as a footballer, I'd say the most important thing is to practise your skills a lot. But as well as that you need to really enjoy your football - I'd say that's the main thing!"

FOOTY WORDSEARCH!

It's time to test your footy knowledge, dudes! Can you find the 50 Prem stars hiding in this massive word jumble?

```
H L X Y D M X V S E S T G S N Z C O R L U K A J O W B B G K Z
J T P O Y T Q G I O B Z F C O N R V T B B A Z B X V N T U J G
W I L H E L M S S O N H Y K S E H C N O K A G F J B I B A E H
R S O S N O L A L W W T D D D O N O I O I K C G O J E K K L C
F I S E V S Y Y D D A I R G R R E W D T S D K O E W M P J M U
L D R R J U O P Z V S G H Q A H S E L K E C J H D R I V A H O
T W W U E Q U J E T P A P L H H L W K O N X X A C J B L A P R
J E K O H T N J I V A Z Z W C C E C H L O E Z V U Y O T U Q C
J L M I R U G N K X R F S K I A N Y T Y J I A G I U C Y A U K
O L O M J D T I V I N F I L R E B E S A G N A T D H H A M W I
G A T F M E L E R N A L N D N A Y C R A U J O A Z I I L E H K
J K J T S A O T W I B M J M Z X N D O O W E R A H O I C O A S
X L Y I O F M F X M Y I N N A V O E G Z O E X R R M I N B R R
A E P C Z U U H U A Q P J B S I M R N H A M Q K I U R X I G E
A I V H W B R X T L U O U R E I I C P R K Y N F X T A S Y R I
C G I F I N F E A F E T Y A N M P V N V A O E B T O T E W E B
P A D F F E V B A G U O L M R V B S X B P A L O B R N R B A I
A J U Q E V T L R N D V A B A I H P K H O H C A A R U R Q V S
R V K I Q I D T A F R V E L B A N A U G F V P T R A M O S E M
K Z A J I L Q P B Y U P H E W U R E N D R A G E T Z U T I S F
E Q G U W L E Q T U E Y P K P W B Y B E N T F N O I L T D P A
R I O C V E E G A V A S A M H C A H I L L W Y G N P Y M H L G
M Y A C N U T Q L E B A B W N O Z J T W R A I Z U N D T R Q W
```

- AGGER
- ALONSO
- AMEOBI
- BABEL
- BARNES
- BARTON
- BENT
- BOATENG
- BRAMBLE
- CAHILL
- CECH
- CORLUKA
- CROUCH
- DISTIN
- EARNSHAW
- ETUHU
- FAE

MY SCORE /50

- FLAMINI
- GARDNER
- GEOVANNI
- HAREWOOD
- HARGREAVES
- HEALY
- JAGIELKA
- JONES
- KAPO
- KONCHESKY
- MALOUDA
- MOORE
- MUNTARI
- NELSEN
- NEVILLE
- NIEMI
- PARKER

ANSWERS ON PAGE 92!

- PARNABY
- PIZARRO
- QUEUDRUE
- RICHARDSON
- RIGTERS
- SAGNA
- SAVAGE
- SIBIERSKI
- SIDWELL
- TAARABT
- TORRES
- TOURE
- TUNCAY
- VIDUKA
- WILHELMSSON
- YOUNG

MATCH!

FACT FILE!

CLUB: Valencia

POSITION: Striker **AGE:** 31

TROPHY COUNT – 11:
3 Champions League, 2 La Liga, 2 Spanish Super Cup, 2 Intercontinental Cup, 1 FA Cup & 1 European Super Cup.

BOOTS:
Adidas +Predator Absolute.

CHAMPO LEAGUE FACT: He's the only player to have scored Champions League goals for four clubs – Real, Monaco, Liverpool and Valencia!

FERNANDO MORIENTES

WAYNE ROONEY'S

Wayne Rooney is one of the biggest stars on the planet! The striker has scored loads of wicked goals and played in some mega games. Check out his super scrapbook...

2000: ENGLAND SUPERKID!

Wayne Rooney started to become a big star in the England youth teams! Even back then, he loved playing for his country!

MAY 2002: YOUTH CUP ACTION!

Wayne scored loads of goals as Everton reached the FA Youth Cup final! He scored in the final, but The Toffees lost 4-2 on aggregate to Aston Villa!

AUGUST 2002: EVERTON DEBUT!

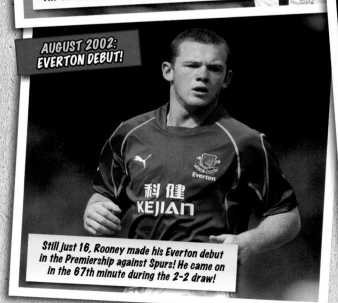

Still just 16, Rooney made his Everton debut in the Premiership against Spurs! He came on in the 67th minute during the 2-2 draw!

OCTOBER 2002: WONDERGOAL!

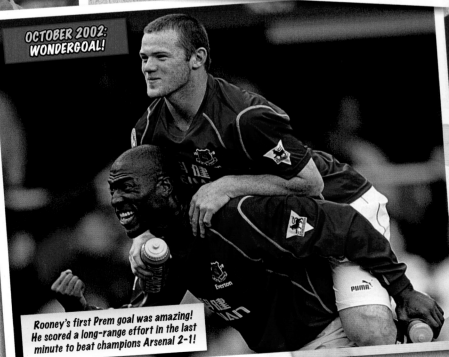

Rooney's first Prem goal was amazing! He scored a long-range effort in the last minute to beat champions Arsenal 2-1!

SCRAPBOOK!

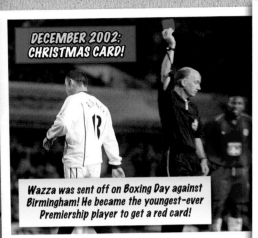

DECEMBER 2002: CHRISTMAS CARD!

Wazza was sent off on Boxing Day against Birmingham! He became the youngest-ever Premiership player to get a red card!

FEBRUARY 2003: ENGLAND DEBUT!

Roo made his England debut against Australia! He became his country's youngest-ever star at just 17 years and 111 days old!

AUGUST 2003: MATCH MATE!

Wayne was well happy to pick up his first MATCH award! He won best Young Gun and Goal Of The Season!

SEPTEMBER 2003: GOAL KING!

Against Macedonia in 2003, he scored his first goal for England! It set The Three Lions on their way to a vital 2-1 win!

FEBRUARY 2004: DOUBLE STRIKE!

After going ten games without a goal, Rooney hit back with a cool double at Southampton!

JUNE 2004: EURO HERO!

Rooney was magic at the Euro 2004 finals! He scored four goals in the first three games - suddenly he was a worldwide superstar!

JUNE 2004: THE PAIN GAME!

Oh no! The striker broke his foot in the Euro 2004 quarter-final as England lost to Portugal!

WAYNE ROONEY'S SCRAPBOOK!

AUGUST 2004: RED DEVIL ROONEY!

HOME TEAM

Man. United splashed out £30 million to buy Rooney from Everton! It was a world record for a teenager and the United fans were well happy!

SEPTEMBER 2004: HAT-TRICK HERO!

After recovering from his foot injury, Wayne smashed in a stunning hat-trick in his first-ever game for Man. United!

OCTOBER 2004: BIRTHDAY STRIKE!

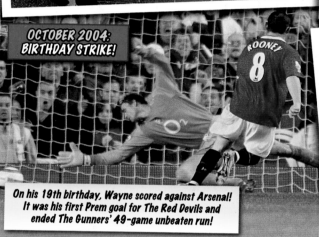

On his 19th birthday, Wayne scored against Arsenal! It was his first Prem goal for The Red Devils and ended The Gunners' 49-game unbeaten run!

THANK YOU FOR ROONEY!

NOVEMBER 2004: FIFA FOOTY STAR!

Wayne became the star of the FIFA footy games!

JANUARY 2005: ANFIELD GLORY!

The dynamite striker loved scoring the winner for United against Liverpool - his big rivals when he played for Everton!

APRIL 2005: PFA WINNER!

The 19-year-old won the PFA Young Player Of The Year award! The cool trophy is voted for by all the other Premiership stars!

MAY 2005: CUP FINAL LOSER!

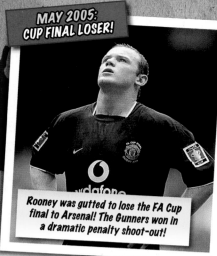

Rooney was gutted to lose the FA Cup final to Arsenal! The Gunners won in a dramatic penalty shoot-out!

JUNE 2005: AWARDS TIME!

Wayne scooped more MATCH awards! He won Young Player Of The Season and Goal Of The Season in our readers' poll!

AUGUST 2005: GOODISON GOAL!

When the new season kicked off, he scored in United's first game – against his old club Everton!

FEBRUARY 2006: MEDAL MAN!

Roo won his first trophy! He scored twice in the 4-0 Carling Cup final win over Wigan and was Man Of The Match, too!

APRIL 2006: INJURY STRIKES!

Wayne broke his foot against Chelsea! It left him in a race to be fit for the World Cup finals!

JUNE 2006: WORLD CUP WOE!

Wayne was fit to play at the World Cup, but he didn't score a goal and was sent off against Portugal in the quarter-final!

WAYNE'S WONDER STRIKES!

England 6-1 Iceland
June 5, 2004

Rooney scored a cracker in this friendly for England! He rocketed the ball in from 25 yards and made it look well easy!

Man. United 2-1 Portsmouth
January 27, 2007

The striker's clever chip over Portsmouth goalkeeper David James in the fourth round of the FA Cup was amazing!

Man. United 2-1 Newcastle
April 24, 2005

This blockbuster nearly broke the net! Wayne's wicked volley against Newcastle in the Prem was one of his best goals ever!

Leeds 0-1 Everton
November 3, 2002

In his first season at Everton, this beauty from the edge of the box helped The Toffees beat Leeds in the Prem at Elland Road!

Arsenal 2-1 Everton
March 23, 2003

The Everton wonderkid scored against Prem champs Arsenal at Highbury! His low shot into the bottom corner was unstoppable!

WAYNE ROONEY'S SCRAPBOOK!

AUGUST 2006: FIRST-DAY DOUBLE!

Rooney roared back into action in the 2006-07 season! He smashed in two goals as The Red Devils thumped Fulham 5-1!

OCTOBER 2006: BOLTON BLITZED!

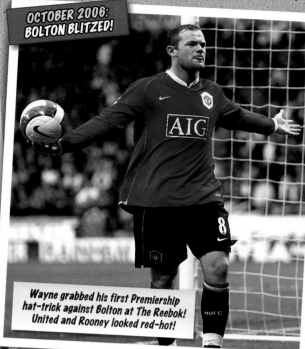

Wayne grabbed his first Premiership hat-trick against Bolton at The Reebok! United and Rooney looked red-hot!

OCTOBER 2006: HAPPY 21ST!

The striker hooked up with his fave footy mag to celebrate his 21st birthday!

NOVEMBER 2006: DUTCH DESTROYER!

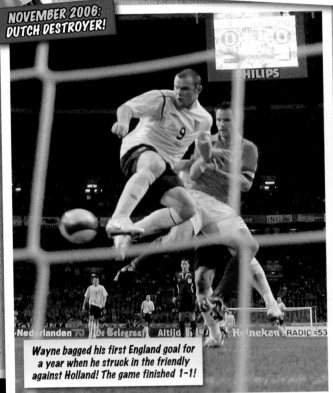

Wayne bagged his first England goal for a year when he struck in the friendly against Holland! The game finished 1-1!

APRIL 2007: ROMA ROMP!

United beat Roma 8-3 on aggregate in the Champo League quarter-finals – and Wazza scored in both games!

APRIL 2007: MILAN MISERY!

Rooney scored twice in the first leg of the Champions League semis against AC Milan, but United crashed out 5-3 on aggregate!

MAY 2007: TITLE PARTY!

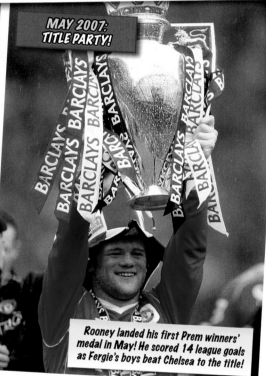

Rooney landed his first Prem winners' medal in May! He scored 14 league goals as Fergie's boys beat Chelsea to the title!

MAY 2007: CUP RUNNER-UP!

It was bad luck again for Wayne in the FA Cup final! Man. United lost 1-0 to Chelsea in extra-time!

JULY 2007: TOP TEN!

At the start of the 2007-08 season, Wayne was given the famous No.10 shirt at Man. United!

WAYNE ROONEY: THE FUTURE!

He's had a wicked career so far, and we reckon he's gonna get better and better! Watch out for Wazza!

WAYNE'S WONDER STRIKES!

Croatia 2-4 England
June 21, 2004

At the Euro 2004 finals, Wazza's thunder strike from outside the box flew past the Croatia 'keeper!

Everton 2-1 Aston Villa
April 26, 2003

This crisp left-foot volley from the edge of the box sent the fans wild! It was in the 89th minute and gave Everton all three points!

Charlton 2-2 Everton
August 26, 2003

Wayne controlled a cross in the box, brought the ball down and banged a left-foot rocket into the roof of the net!

Man. United 3-0 Middlesbrough
January 29, 2005

This volley in the FA Cup was awesome! Rooney blasted a rasping right-footer past Boro 'keeper Mark Schwarzer!

Watford 1-4 Man. United
April 14, 2007

The striker collected the ball on the edge of the box and powered a beauty into the top corner after just seven minutes!

LIGUE 1 QUIZ!

Can you answer these ten rock-hard questions about the awesome French top flight? It's well tough!

1

Bolo Zenden left Liverpool to join which massive club?

2

Who are the Ligue 1 champs?

3

Which SPL side did PSG boss Paul Le Guen used to manage?

4

Which Ligue 1 team play at the wicked Stade Louis II stadium?

5

Which French team wears this cool kit - PSG or Lille?

6
Which top defender moved from Auxerre to Arsenal this summer?

7

Name this ace Marseille star!

MY SCORE /10

8

How many league titles have St. Etienne won - eight, ten or 12?

9

Which Ligue 1 club did Chelsea sign Florent Malouda from?

10

True or False? Lens won the UEFA Cup in 2005.

ANSWERS ON PAGE 92!

WONDERKIDZ 2008
REVEALED!

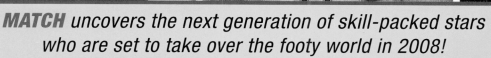
MATCH uncovers the next generation of skill-packed stars who are set to take over the footy world in 2008!

TURN THE PAGE TO SEE EUROPE'S BEST NEW TALENT!

EUROPE!

HE'S THE NEW...
MICHAEL ESSIEN

DANNY ROSE

CLUB: Tottenham
COUNTRY: England
POSITION: Midfielder
AGE: 17

The England Under-17 midfielder loves getting on the ball and starting attacking moves. His charging runs and defence-splitting passes are pure gold!

VICTOR MOSES

CLUB: Crystal Palace
COUNTRY: England
POSITION: Striker
AGE: 16

Put together power, pace and a hunger for goals and you get Victor Moses! The Crystal Palace striker will rip up the Championship this season!

HE'S THE NEW...
WAYNE ROONEY

BOJAN KRKIC

CLUB: Barcelona
COUNTRY: Spain
POSITION: Striker
AGE: 17

The teenage goal machine has what it takes to become a true Spanish footy great! His close control, vision and deadly finishing are already top class!

HE'S THE NEW...
THIERRY HENRY

FRAN MERIDA

CLUB: Arsenal
COUNTRY: Spain
POSITION: Attacking midfielder
AGE: 17

Arsenal got a mega bargain when they snapped up Merida from Barcelona last summer! His skills on the ball and shots from long distance are well wicked!

HE'S THE NEW...
ARJEN ROBBEN

TODAY'S TOP WONDERKIDS!

Try to name these wicked young stars who hit the big-time in 2007!

CLUB: Arsenal   **COUNTRY:** England
ANSWER

CLUB: Liverpool   **COUNTRY:** Denmark
ANSWER

CLUB: Roma   **COUNTRY:** Italy
ANSWER

HE'S THE NEW...
STEVEN GERRARD

JEFFREY SARPONG

CLUB: Ajax
COUNTRY: Holland
POSITION: Attacking midfielder
AGE: 19

Ajax fans aren't missing Wesley Sneijder this season because they've got Jeffrey Sarpong! The 19-year-old is a midfield master with awesome passing skills!

IGOR AKINFEEV

CLUB: CSKA Moscow
COUNTRY: Russia
POSITION: Goalkeeper
AGE: 21

Akinfeev may be only 21 but he's already the CSKA Moscow and Russia No.1! He loves catching crosses and hardly ever makes the wrong decision!

HE'S THE NEW...
PETR CECH

HE'S THE NEW...
CRISTIANO RONALDO

SAMIR NASRI

CLUB: Marseille
COUNTRY: France
POSITION: Winger
AGE: 20

There aren't many better sights in world footy than Samir Nasri running with the ball! He's lightning-quick and he's got more tricks than most magicians!

TURN OVER TO SEE SOUTH AMERICA'S YOUNG STARS!

CLUB: Arsenal ✕ **COUNTRY:** Spain
ANSWER

CLUB: Tottenham ✕ **COUNTRY:** Wales
ANSWER

CLUB: Man. City ✕ **COUNTRY:** England
ANSWER

CLUB: Ajax ✕ **COUNTRY:** Holland
ANSWER

SOUTH AMERICA!

RENATO AUGUSTO

CLUB: Flamengo
COUNTRY: Brazil
POSITION: Midfielder
AGE: 19

Augusto loves mixing it up with the toughest defenders in the Brazilian league! He's also dangerous around the box where he loves hitting ace curlers!

HE'S THE NEW...
RIVALDO

FRANCO DI SANTO

HE'S THE NEW...
PETER CROUCH

CLUB: Audax Italiano
COUNTRY: Argentina
POSITION: Striker
AGE: 18

At 193cms tall, Di Santo is a massive talent in more ways than one! He's very good in the air, but his tricky feet mean he's handy on the ground too!

SERGIO AGUERO

CLUB: Atletico Madrid
COUNTRY: Argentina
POSITION: Striker
AGE: 19

Sergio Aguero was born a footy genius! He can lose a man-marker in a second, before sprinting 30 yards and firing the perfect finish into the net. He rocks!

HE'S THE NEW...
CARLOS TEVEZ

ARTURO VIDAL

CLUB: Bayer Leverkusen
COUNTRY: Chile
POSITION: Defender
AGE: 20

Vidal is a shut-out master! He forms a brick wall in front of goal that strikers can't get past, before winning the ball and starting an attack for his team!

HE'S THE NEW...
ROBERTO AYALA

TODAY'S TOP WONDERKIDS!

Try to name these wicked young stars who hit the big-time in 2007!

CLUB: Werder Bremen ★ **COUNTRY:** Brazil
ANSWER

CLUB: Man. United ★ **COUNTRY:** Argentina
ANSWER

CLUB: PSV Eindhoven ★ **COUNTRY:** Peru
ANSWER

HE'S THE NEW... RONALDINHO

LULINHA

CLUB: Corinthians
COUNTRY: Brazil
POSITION: Attacking midfielder
AGE: 17

Lulinha loves playing in the hole behind the strikers, where he picks up the ball and dances his way past defenders before firing off a shot or killer pass!

ALEXANDRE PATO

CLUB: AC Milan
COUNTRY: Brazil
POSITION: Striker
AGE: 18

AC Milan won the race to sign Pato, or 'The Duck' as he's also known, last summer. His unselfish play means he sets up as many goals as he scores!

HE'S THE NEW... ZLATAN IBRAHIMOVIC

HE'S THE NEW... MICHAEL OWEN

LUIS SUAREZ

CLUB: Ajax
COUNTRY: Uruguay
POSITION: Striker
AGE: 20

Ajax paid £5 million to sign the Uruguay youngster last summer. He loves chasing balls over the top of defences before jinking round the 'keeper to bag a goal!

TURN THE PAGE FOR MORE AWESOME WONDERKIDS!

CLUB: *Real Madrid* ★ COUNTRY: *Argentina*
ANSWER

CLUB: *Man. United* ★ COUNTRY: *Brazil*
ANSWER

CLUB: *Barcelona* ★ COUNTRY: *Argentina*
ANSWER

CLUB: *Arsenal* ★ COUNTRY: *Brazil*
ANSWER

WONDERKIDZ 2008! WONDERKIDZ 2008!

THE REST OF THE

NORTH AMERICA

DANNY SZETELA

CLUB: Columbus Crew
COUNTRY: USA
POSITION: Midfielder
AGE: 20

Danny shot to fame after scoring three goals for the USA at the World Under-20 Championships last summer! He's big and strong and knows where the goal is!

HE'S THE NEW...
LUCA TONI

GIOVANNI DOS SANTOS

CLUB: Barcelona
COUNTRY: Mexico
POSITION: Winger
AGE: 18

There's no way of knowing where Dos Santos will go or what he'll do when he's running at you with the ball! His footwork and ball skills are amazing!

HE'S THE NEW...
FRANCESCO TOTTI

HE'S THE NEW...
SAMUEL ETO'O

BABACAR GUEYE

CLUB: Metz
COUNTRY: Senegal
POSITION: Striker
AGE: 21

Gueye's non-stop running and rocket shots made the Senegal striker a huge success in the French league in 2007. Expect more of the same in 2008!

TODAY'S TOP WONDERKIDS!

Try to name these wicked young stars who hit the big-time in 2007!

CLUB: Chelsea ★ **COUNTRY:** Nigeria
ANSWER

CLUB: Benfica ★ **COUNTRY:** USA
ANSWER

CLUB: Chelsea ★ **COUNTRY:** Ivory Coast
ANSWER

WORLD!

AFRICA

HE'S THE NEW...
ALESSANDRO NESTA

NATHAN BURNS

CLUB: Adelaide United
COUNTRY: Australia
POSITION: Striker
AGE: 19

Loads of European clubs are ready to bid for the Adelaide United trickster. His weaving runs and smart finishing are causing chaos in Australia's A League!

HE'S THE NEW...
MARK VIDUKA

KANG MIN-SOO

CLUB: Chunnam Dragons
COUNTRY: South Korea
POSITION: Defender
AGE: 21

Min-Soo is one of the best defenders in Asia! His razor-sharp footy brain helps him sniff out trouble before it happens and he's pretty quick off the mark, too!

ASIA

HE'S THE NEW...
PATRICK VIEIRA

HE'S THE NEW...
RONALDO

TAKAYUKI MORIMOTO

CLUB: Catania
COUNTRY: Japan
POSITION: Striker
AGE: 19

The Japan ace scored his first Serie A goal for Catania in Italy last season and should be a big player for them in 2008! He's strong, direct and deadly!

EZEKIEL BALA

CLUB: Lyn Oslo
COUNTRY: Nigeria
POSITION: Midfielder
AGE: 20

The ace Nigeria Under-20 captain can play either as an attacking or defensive midfielder. He's got bags of energy and a cannon of a right foot, too. Wicked!

Check out wicked videos of the 2008 wonderkids at www. matchmag.co.uk!

CLUB: *Everton* ✵ **COUNTRY:** *Nigeria*
ANSWER

CLUB: *Udinese* ✵ **COUNTRY:** *Ghana*
ANSWER

CLUB: *Espanyol* ✵ **COUNTRY:** *Cameroon*
ANSWER

ANSWERS

1. Theo Walcott; 2. Daniel Agger; 3. Alberto Aquilani; 4. Cesc Fabregas; 5. Gareth Bale; 6. Micah Richards; 7. Hedwiges Maduro; 8. Diego; 9. Carlos Tevez; 10. Jefferson Farfan; 11. Fernando Gago; 12. Anderson; 13. Lionel Messi; 14. Denilson; 15. John Obi Mikel; 16. Freddy Adu; 17. Salomon Kalou; 18. Victor Anichebe; 19. Asamoah Gyan; 20. Carlos Kameni.

TOTAL /20

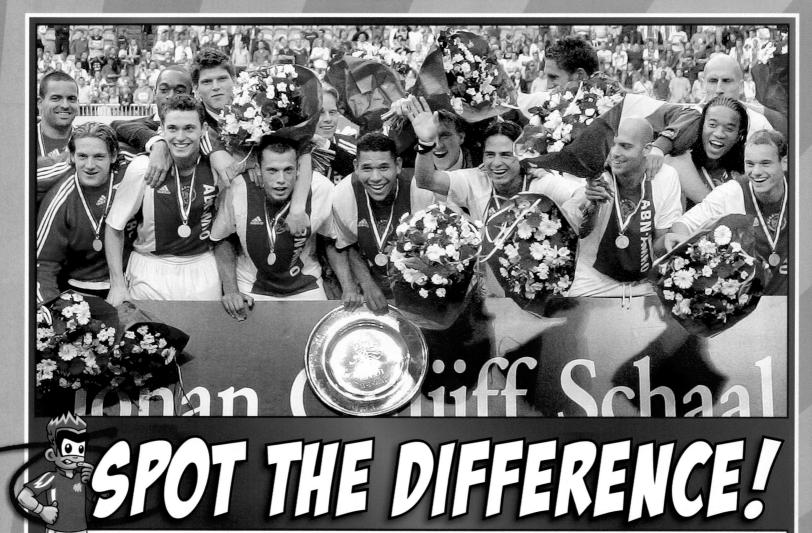

SPOT THE DIFFERENCE!

Can you spot all five differences between these two pics of Dutch giants Ajax? Two points for each correct answer!

MY SCORE /10

ANSWERS ON PAGE 92!

MATCH!

CHAMPO LEAGUE STARS!

JUNINHO

FACT FILE!

CLUB: Lyon

POSITION: Midfielder **AGE:** 32

TROPHY COUNT – 13: 6 Ligue 1, 4 Trophee Des Champions, 2 Brazilian Championship & 1 Copa Libertadores.

BOOTS:
Adidas +Predator Absolute.

CHAMPO LEAGUE FACT:
Set-piece king Juninho scored four free-kicks in the 2005-06 Champions League campaign!

SUPER Seas

61

62
Get in! Your boys lift
the FA Cup at Wembley!
Move to square 65!

63

Disaster! Two team-mates
have a scrap on the pitch
and both get red-carded!
Miss a turn!

64

65

60
You take your players to a
training camp in Spain!
Forward one square!

59

58

57
Gutted! Your captain's gonna
retire at the end of the season!
Miss a turn!

56

41

42

You bring in two
class new players
during the transfer window!
Roll again!

43

44
Your team get an easy
draw in the FA Cup!
Move forward one square!

45

40

39
The team bounce back from
their shock Carling Cup exit
with another win in Europe!
Move forward two squares!

38

37
Bad times! Your team
crashes out of the Carling Cup
to a well rubbish League 2 side!
Miss a turn!

36

21

22

23

24
Your team win their first
Champions League match!
Roll again!

25

20

19

18
Kanye West says he
supports your team!
Move to square 22!

17

16
Roll more than three and
you move forward ten spaces!
Get less than a three and you
miss a turn. Nightmare!

START
Roll one
dice to
start!

2

3

Your goalkeeper
gets injured during
a pre-season friendly!
Go back to the start!

4

5
Wow! Your team
gets a well flash kit
for the new season!
Move forward two squares!

ON GAME!

66 The Champions League final goes to penalties! Roll higher than a three to win and get another turn!

67

68

69 It's the last game of the season! Roll an even number to move forward – an odd number sends you back to square 64!

FINISH You've done it! Another wicked season is over and your trophy cabinet is loaded with silverware!

55 Get in! Your team win their Champions League semi-final! Move forward one square!

54

53 Your silky winger ruins everything by going on Celebrity Big Brother. Doh! Go back to square 48!

52

51

46

47 Your top striker brings out a rubbish rap song! Go back one square!

48

49

50 Matchmag.co.uk readers vote you the top manager in the Prem! Go to square 52!

35 Ouch! Your captain picks up a nasty injury! Go back two squares!

34

33

32

31

26

27 Oh no! Heavy rain floods your stadium! Go back one square!

28

29

30 You thrash your local rivals 5-0 in a massive derby match! Move forward to square 33!

15

14

13 Oh no! Chelsea nick your best defender! Go back to square seven!

12

11

6

7

8 Get in! The gaffer buys a top striker! Take an extra turn!

9 EDUARDO 9

10

QUIZ ANSWERS!

★ QUIZ 1 PAGE 36! ★

LA LIGA QUIZ!

1	Valencia
2	Bernd Schuster
3	Atletico Madrid
4	Athletic Bilbao
5	Santiago Canizares
6	True
7	Sevilla
8	Portugal
9	Andriy Shevchenko
10	Celta Vigo

MY SCORE: /10

★ QUIZ 2 PAGE 44! ★

WORDFIT!

MY SCORE: /50

★ QUIZ 3 PAGE 48! ★

SERIE A QUIZ!

1	Francesco Totti
2	Seven
3	Palermo
4	Adriano
5	Claudio Ranieri
6	True
7	99
8	Fiorentina
9	France
10	San Siro

MY SCORE: /10

★ QUIZ 4 PAGE 56! ★

SPOT THE STARS!

1	Teddy Sheringham
2	Robbie Fowler
3	Paddy Kenny
4	Marlon King
5	Jon Stead
6	Matt Holland
7	Bruno N'Gotty
8	Kevin Phillips
9	Darren Huckerby
10	Arjan De Zeeuw

MY SCORE: /10

> ADD UP YER MARKS TO SEE HOW YOU'VE DONE!

MY SCORE: /160

0-50! — **REALLY RUBBISH!**
Keep reading MATCH to boost your footy knowledge!

51-100! — **PRETTY GOOD!**
You know your Carragher from your Carew!

101-160! — **AWESOME!**
What a great effort, you're a footy genius!

★ QUIZ 5 PAGE 64! ★

BUNDESLIGA QUIZ!

1	Stuttgart
2	Sweden
3	The Allianz Arena
4	Borussia Dortmund
5	Hamburg
6	Luca Toni
7	Second
8	Eintracht Frankfurt
9	True
10	Aston Villa

MY SCORE: /10

★ QUIZ 6 PAGE 72! ★

FOOTY WORDSEARCH!

```
HLXYDMXVSESTGSNZCORLUKAJOWBBGKZ
JTPOYTQGIOBZFCONRVTBBAZBXVNTUJG
WILHELMSSONHYKSEHCNOKAGFJBIBAEH
RSOSNOLALWWTDDDONOIOIKCGOJEKKLU
FISEVSYYDDARGPRREWDTSDKOEWMPJMU
TWWUEQUJETPAPLHHLWKONXXXAJBLAPR
JEKOHTNJIVAZZWCCECHLOEZVUYOTUQC
JLMIRJGNKXRFSKIANYTYJIAGIUCYAUK
OLOMJDTIVINFILREBESAGNATDHHAMWI
GATFMELERNALNDNAYCRAUJOAZILEHK
JKKJTSAOTWIBMJMZXNDOOWERAHOICOAS
XLYIOWPRXTLUOUENJTKXMYINNAVOEGZ
AEPCZUUHUAQPJBSIMRNHAMQKIURXIGE
AIVHWBRXTLUOUENJTKXMYINNAVOEGZ
CGIFINFEAFETYANMPVNVAOEBTOTEWEB
PADFFEVBAGUOLMRVBSXBPALOBRNRBAR
RVKIQIDTAFRVELBANAUGFVPTRAMOSEM
KZAJILQPBYUPHEWURENDRAGETZUTISP
EQGUWLEQTUEYPKPWBYBENTFNOILTDPA
RIOCVEEGAVASAMHCAHILLWYGNPYMHLG
MYACNUTQLEBABWNOZJTWRAIZUNDTRQW
```

MY SCORE: /50

★ QUIZ 7 PAGE 80! ★

LIGUE 1 QUIZ!

1	Marseille
2	Lyon
3	Rangers
4	Monaco
5	PSG
6	Bacary Sagna
7	Djibril Cisse
8	Ten
9	Lyon
10	False

MY SCORE: /10

★ QUIZ 8 PAGE 88! ★

SPOT THE DIFFERENCE!

1	Medal from third player in from the left has disappeared.
2	Player in the top right of picture has disappeared.
3	Player second from the left's shorts are now red.
4	Bunch of flowers at the very back have disappeared.
5	Sponsor on player's shirt second in from right shirt has disappeared.

MY SCORE: /10

MATCH!

CHAMPO LEAGUE STARS!

FACT FILE!

CLUB: Celtic

POSITION: Midfielder **AGE:** 29

TROPHY COUNT – 6:
2 Scottish Premier League,
1 Scottish Cup, 1 Scottish
League Cup, 1 J. League
& 1 J. League Cup.

BOOTS: Adidas +F50.

CHAMPO LEAGUE FACT:
The awesome Japan midfielder
scored two wicked free-kicks
against Man. United in last
season's Champions League!

SHUNSUKE NAKAMURA

FINAL WHISTLE!

NICE ONE, YOU'VE REACHED THE END OF THE 2008 MATCH ANNUAL!

GREAT WORK, FELLA!

BACK OF THE NET!

YOU'RE A REAL FOOTY FAN!

10 THINGS TO DO IN... 2008!

1 GO TO A GAME!
Go with your mates to watch a live game of footy! You'll love the red-hot action in front of you!

2 LEARN NEW SKILLS!
Boost your footy powers on the pitch! Coach King gives you top tips every week in MATCH! Don't miss it!

3 WEAR THE SHIRT!
If you wanna support your team, it's well cool to wear the shirt so everyone knows who you follow!

4 STICK UP POSTERS!
There are loads of wicked posters in MATCH every week! Stick your faves on your bedroom wall!

EVERTON
PHIL JAGIELKA

5 TV TUNE-IN!
There are no end of top games on the box, so park up on the sofa, relax and enjoy the big match!

6 CLEAN YOUR BOOTS!
You can't play footy with muddy boots! Give 'em a good scrub every week!

7 VISIT THE WICKED WEBSITE!
The MATCH website rocks! Log on to www.matchmag.co.uk every day!

I feel like dancing!

8 COPY THE STARS!
When you score a goal for your team, pull off a crazy celebration just like the stars do on the pitch!

9 CHECK OUT EURO 2008!
Catch all the action from the biggest tournament this summer!

10 READ MATCH!
MATCH is the No.1 footy mag on the planet, so make sure you snap it up every single Tuesday!

BUST THE NET!

SEE YA, FOOTY FANS!
We hope you've enjoyed the 2008 MATCH Annual! Keep reading the mag!